PREACHING
and the literary forms of the Bible

PREACHING
and the literary forms of the Bible

THOMAS G. LONG

FORTRESS PRESS   PHILADELPHIA

*To Lon and Lib
who know how
to give a blessing.*

Library of Congress Cataloging-in-Publication Data

Long, Thomas G., 1946–
  Preaching and the literary forms of the Bible.

  Bibliography: p.
  Inclues index.
  1. Bible—Homiletical use. I. Title.
  BS534.5.L66 1989   251   88-45243
  ISBN 0-8006-2313-4

Printed in the U.S.A.   1-2313

                                        13   14   15

contents

preface

There are constraints which shadow interpretation;
and the first is genre.
Frank Kermode, *The Genesis of Secrecy*

This investigation into the relationship between the literary genres in the Bible and Christian preaching has carried me deep into the territories of biblical and literary criticism, lands for which I carry no portfolio and where I can barely speak the native tongues. Experts will instantly spot me as a tourist, and I can only hope that they will tolerate my blunders while enjoying my appreciative wonder over what I have seen.

I am especially mindful of how deeply those who preach have always depended upon the labors of biblical scholars. Serious preaching simply could not occur were it not for their work. I am bold enough to believe, though, that biblical scholarship gains both energy and focus through the urgings and promptings of preachers. The preacher does not merely sit in the waiting room of the biblical scholar, patiently biding time until the door finally opens and the latest batch of findings is announced. The issue raised by preaching is not how to *use*, in a popular way, the gleanings of biblical study but the more central issue of how to *approach* the Bible in the first place. The act of preaching in and for the church presents exegetical and hermeneutical questions in pointed and urgent ways, and these questions are sometimes different and, in a way, more demanding than those raised by the academy. The best biblical scholarship, I am convinced, is done by those who work while hearing the sound of the preacher, concerned about next Sunday's sermon, knocking on the study door.

My deepest gratitude is extended to those biblical scholars whose work is cited in this book. I pray that they will find themselves treated fairly, even where there are points of disagreement between us, and that they will be encouraged by the sound of this preacher's knock on their door.

THOMAS G. LONG
Princeton, New Jersey

Part 1

THE APPROACH

1
LEARNING
how to read

PREACHING AND BIBLICAL
LITERARY FORMS

This book is about biblical preaching, and it is based upon the relatively simple idea that the literary form and dynamics of a biblical text can and should be important factors in the preacher's navigation of the distance between text and sermon. Preachers who have sought to be open and attentive to biblical texts in their preaching have long sensed that a sermon based upon a psalm, for example, ought somehow to be different from one that grows out of a miracle story, not only because of *what* the two texts say but also because of *how* the texts say what they say. A psalm is poetry, a miracle story is narrative; and because they are two distinct literary and rhetorical forms, they "come at" the reader in different ways and create contrasting effects. What is needed, then, is a process of sermon development sufficiently nuanced to recognize and employ these differences in the creation of the sermon itself.

In recent years, this feeling has increasingly found support in biblical scholarship. More and more, biblical scholars have augmented the methods of textual interpretation to include literary and rhetorical approaches, thereby expanding both the avenues of access to biblical texts and the range of possibilities for hearing the claims of those texts upon contemporary life. This book attempts to incorporate some of these approaches and the wealth of insight they bring into the methods of biblical preaching.

I will not attempt to address every important issue in biblical preaching. There are already many good discussions of such matters as the authority of Scripture and lectionary preaching. Moreover, the case for biblical preaching itself has been ably presented by others. I will focus instead on one underdeveloped aspect of biblical preaching: the role that literary forms such as proverb, narrative, psalm, and parable can play in the creation of sermons. It is particularly crucial that preachers give attention to biblical literary form and dynamics because these are precisely the aspects of biblical texts commonly washed out in the typical text-to-sermon process. It is ironic that preachers often disregard these dimensions of a text since attention to these "textual poetics" brings us into contact with what resonates most harmoniously with a key ingredient in the homiletical task: deciding how to preach so that the sermon embodies in its language, form, and style the gospel it seeks to proclaim.

The writers of Scripture faced a communication problem similar to the one encountered by the contemporary preacher—finding the most effective rhetorical shape for their messages. Recent biblical scholarship has, in fact, been attentive to the many rhetorical strategies the early writers employed. Nonetheless, while there is an abundance of talk in the preaching literature about the use of images, plots, arguments, and poetic devices, as they appear within *sermons*, there is not much help about what sense or use to make of those very same elements when they appear in the *texts* from which those sermons spring.

An unfortunate result of overlooking the literary properties of biblical texts is the tendency to view those texts by default as inert containers for theological concepts. The preacher's task then becomes simply throwing the text into an exegetical winepress, squeezing out the ideational matter, and then figuring out homiletical ways to make those ideas attractive to contemporary listeners. The literary and rhetorical shape of the texts matters not at all; it is discarded as ornament.

The mistake in this, of course, is that the literary dimensions of texts are not merely decorative. Texts are not packages containing ideas; they are means of communication. When we ask ourselves what a text means, we are not searching for the *idea* of the text. We are trying to discover its total impact upon a reader—and everything about a text works together to create that impact. We may casually speak of the form and the content of a text as if they were two separate realities, but if "content" is used as a synonym for "meaning,"

the form must be seen as a vital part of the content. Perhaps it would
be more accurate to speak of the *form of the content.*

Two biblical texts may share the same theological theme but by
virtue of different literary dynamics do quite different things with
that common conceptual core. For instance, Matt. 24:43-44 and 2
Peter 3:10 appear at first glance to be renditions of the same idea.
They share the same theological theme—the day of the Lord—and
even employ the same imagery—the surprising arrival of a thief.
They are, in other words, speaking about the same issue and using
the same terminology. Despite these similarities, however, the texts
are expressions of two different literary forms and thus cannot be
blended exegetically or homiletically into one. They function quite
differently since one occurs as part of a synoptic discourse and the
other as part of an epistolary argument. Careful readers of the passages experience them in quite distinct ways. So what appears at first
glance to be the same idea merely "packaged" in two different literary
shapes turns out, when the effects upon readers are considered, not
to be the same idea after all. It follows, then, that sermons based upon
each of these two passages should reflect this distinction in some
significant way.

The idea that the literary form of a biblical text is hermeneutically
important and should exert influence in the production of a sermon
seems simple enough. Closer scrutiny reveals, however, that this is
actually a rather complex insight bristling with unanswered questions.
What *is* literary form? Precisely what relationship does literary form
have to what is typically called "meaning" in biblical texts? When and
how, in the process of moving from text to sermon, should the literary
dynamics of a text be taken into account? What is the connection
between an approach to texts that focuses upon literary form and
dynamics and the more traditional approaches to biblical exegesis,
such as historical criticism? What linkage should there be between
the form of a text and the structure of a sermon based upon that text?
To answer these questions, we must first examine the basic role form
plays in human communication.

THE FORMFULNESS OF HUMAN COMMUNICATION

Whenever people communicate with each other, they do more than
employ words and gestures. They place those verbal and nonverbal

elements into some kind of recognizable pattern, that is, into a *form*. If I say, "the loves the boy girl," you do not have a clear idea of what I am trying to say, not because you do not know the definitions of the four words I have used, but because I have not placed them into the conventional pattern of a logical sentence. If I revise the order of my words to say, "the boy loves the girl," or "the girl loves the boy," the words form sentences which obey the rules of English syntax and which can be understood immediately.

Put simply, the pattern of communication called a "correct English sentence" forms a kind of agreement between the two of us, actually among all speakers of English. This implicit agreement has become so ingrained in us that outside of classroom exercises in grammar we rarely think about it at all. But the fact is we are members of a language community which has agreed to speak according to certain formal patterns and to listen according to those same patterns. This tacit agreement to form what we say into mutually recognizable patterns is a crucial part of what makes reliable communication possible.

Speakers and hearers, writers and readers meet on common ground defined in part by the mutual agreement that certain forms will govern the communication between them. These forms are not static; they are dynamic. They have parts, but *moving* parts. The form called a "correct English sentence" has parts (nouns, verbs, adjectives), but these parts relate to each other in action-filled ways (verbs *agree* with subjects, adjectives *modify* nouns). To use a metaphor sometimes employed in philosophical linguistics, human communication is a game played according to certain rules. The form is the game itself; the dynamics of the form are the rules. If I am to understand something you say to me, I must obey the rules of the game. And so must you.

KNOWING HOW TO PLAY THE GAMES

This game-playing would be relatively easy if there were only one game to master, but human communication consists of many games played on many levels and with multiple variations. Sometimes we convey direct information to one another in correctly constructed sentences—that is one game. But we also tell stories, sing songs, make puns, recite poetry, crack jokes, pose questions, and use language in countless other ways, each of which involves a separate game with its own rules. Before we can follow the rules, we must know what game is being played. Catching the ball and running as far as I can with it may be a brilliant play in football but a blunder in baseball. If the speaker is playing one game and the listener another, communication breaks down.

When we read the sentence, "I shot him dead because because he was my foe," we can easily determine its meaning. But if we have read the sentence carefully, we also recognize that according to the rules of direct communication an error has been made in its construction— the word "because" appears twice. The repetition is a minor violation but a violation nonetheless of our agreement regarding how sentences are to be built. We know the rules of this game, and two "becauses" in a row is a foul. As direct communication, therefore, this sentence would be clearer if it read, "I shot him dead because he was my foe."

If we learn, however, that this sentence is not a straightforward bit of information at all, but a line in a poem by Thomas Hardy, a different game is announced, one having to do with a certain literary genre; and a different set of rules comes into play. Here is the complete stanza:

> I shot him dead because—
>   Because he was my foe,
> Just so: my foe of course he was;
>   That's clear enough; although[1]

Because we now know that we are playing a different game, we are fairly certain that the repetition of the word "because" is not a mistake at all, but a poetic strategy designed by Hardy to make the reader aware of the speaker's hesitancy and self-doubt about the motivation behind his actions. Indeed, this awareness is reinforced by the rest of the stanza. The game of poetry is played by rules that are similar to, but different in important ways from, the rules that govern direct discourse. Much of poetry's power is related to the tensions between its rules and the rules governing ordinary discourse.

This example demonstrates that in human communication full meaning is created through neither the particular words we use nor the formal patterns into which those words are arranged, but through the interplay of words and patterns as they are experienced by the reader or hearer. Meaning is the product of the interaction between words placed into certain patterns and the expectations of those who hear or read those words. Speakers and authors play various games with words, but if communication is to take place hearers and readers must be drawn into playing the same game. When we watch the evening news we expect the newscaster to operate by the rules of informational communication, and our listening is governed by the rules of that game. If the newscaster uses two "becauses" in a row, we wince at the error and mentally erase one. If, on the other hand, we know we are hearing a poem, we have different expectations. We are listening according to another set of rules, and "because" twice in a row does not make us wince; it makes us ponder.

FORM AND EXPECTATION

I use the term "expectation" here to refer to a person's readiness to read or listen in a particular way, according to one set of rules and procedures and not another. What happens in our heads when we listen to a speech, read the newspaper, or chat with a neighbor is complex and full of mystery. There is much about this we do not yet fathom, but we do know, at least, that listening and reading are not passive activities. When someone says something to us, we are not blank tablets waiting in stillness for their words to be imprinted upon us. Rather, as the person speaks to us, we are equally active, doing something *to* the words that are spoken in order to secure meaning from them. The analogy must not be pressed too far, but in a limited sense human beings are like computers: we are nimble and complex "processors" of words.

The literary critic Stanley Fish, in analyzing the dynamics of reading, has described the actions which the reader performs upon a text as a "set of interpretive strategies."

> Let us suppose that I am reading *Lycidas*. What is it that I am doing? First of all, what I am doing is not "simply reading," an activity in which I do not believe because it implies the possibility of pure (that is, disinterested) perception. Rather, I am proceeding on the basis of . . . interpretive decisions, . . . [and once] these decisions have been made, . . . I am immediately predisposed to perform certain acts, to "find," by looking for, themes, . . . to confer significances, . . . to mark out "formal" units. . . . My disposition to perform these acts (and others; the list is not meant to be exhaustive) constitutes a set of *interpretive strategies*, which, when they are put into execution, become the large act of reading.[2]

In other words, the acts of hearing and reading consist of a set of operations performed upon the text, whether it is oral or written; as we have seen, different forms of communication demand correspondingly different sets of operations. Fish's point is that we make "interpretive decisions" based upon our assumptions about the sort of communication we are receiving, and once those decisions are made, a certain set of operations swings into place. It is this swinging into place that we have called "expectation."

By way of example, consider the following text:

Once upon a time there was a man who lived in a small village. Though his home was humble, and his life simple, he was a collector of fine clocks, and people would travel for many miles to see his rare and wonderful collection. His clocks were indeed splendid, but none was more magnificent than the one which was called the "Angel Clock." It was a very old clock, but no one, not even the man himself, knew just when it was made, or the circumstances of its creation. Its base was of the finest silver; the figures on its face were precious stones. Rising from its top was an angel made from the purest gold. Each quarter hour was marked by the tone of a flawless chime, and, at each hour, the clock sounded music so lovely the man believed it was the very music of heaven.

One night, while the man was sleeping, a thief entered his home and, when the thief departed, he carried with him only one of the man's possessions. It was the "Angel Clock."

THE END

The end? We resist those two words, saying to ourselves, "This cannot be all. There must be more to the story than *that*." Notice, however, what causes us to react this way. We have *assumed* that this is a story. Nobody told us that this is a story; we have arrived at that conclusion on our own and acted toward the text accordingly. To use Fish's language, we have made an "interpretive decision" that this is a story because it looks like a story. Indeed, because of the appearance of the phrase "once upon a time," and the language and form of this text, we have probably concluded that it is a particular kind of story—a folk, or fairy, tale.

Because we have decided that this is a story, we expect the text to behave like a proper story. Without thinking very much about it, we have swung into place a process of reading that among other things expects to find the standard story parts and sequences, such as a beginning, a middle, and an end. This text has a beginning and perhaps the hint of a middle, but there is clearly no end, and therefore the process of reading is frustrated.

It is important to recognize that the process of reading is disturbed not because we know *this* story in advance but because we have a formal expectation about how *every* story, as an example of a stable literary "type," is supposed to develop. We do not create this expectation out of thin air, of course. We gradually build it through our experience with other stories. Literary critic Robert Scholes says,

> Reading is a largely unconscious activity. We can only read a story if we have read enough other stories to understand the basic elements of narrative coding. Our first stories are told or read to us by our parents, or other parental figures, who explain the codes as they go. The ideal reader shares the author's codes and is able to process the text without confusion or delay.[3]

Whether we call it a narrative code, a set of interpretive strategies, or simply expectation, the point is we have built up a story-shaped form, among many other forms, in our reading and hearing repertoire. When we encounter something that we assume to be a story, we bring that form forward and put it into play, expecting a match with the text. Because the text about the clock collector did not fully match our expectation, because it did not move forward to a satisfactory resolution, we cried foul.

But what if the text had been like this?

Littleton (AP) Littleton police reported yesterday that William Archer, a local resident and a collector of antique clocks, was the victim of a burglary Tuesday night.

The thief apparently entered the home while Archer was sleeping. Only one item, a valuable clock, was reported missing. Several dozen other clocks, including some of great value, were not disturbed.

"I am particularly sad to lose that one," Archer said by telephone. "It was my 'Angel Clock,'" he said, referring to the gold figure of an angel which was a feature of the stolen clock.

Investigator John Bowman of the Littleton Police, who is in charge of the case, expressed optimism that the clock would be recovered. "It will be easy to trace," he said. "It is a chiming clock with a silver base, jewels on the face, and, of course, that angel on the top."

Police sources indicated that there are no suspects at the present time.

If the text ends this way, we are neither perturbed nor surprised. We have assumed that this is a newspaper article, and have therefore put into play the process of reading demanded by those expectations. We do not necessarily expect newspaper articles to have plots, so what seemed to be unfinished in story form now appears in news article form to be complete. For a piece of oral or written communication to "work," there must be cooperative interaction between what is said or written and those who read or hear it.

GUESSING GAME

How do we know what to expect from a piece of communication? When we read or listen how do we know to act one way toward one speech or text and another way toward another? Sometimes, of course, we are told in advance what to expect. The speaker begins by saying, "That reminds me of a funny story," or, "Looking now at the weather in the metro area." Such introductions are a kind of instruction to the hearer about how to listen. When the Gospel writer Luke states, "And he told them a parable, to the effect that they ought always to pray and not to lose heart," he is giving the reader both the literary form of what follows and something to watch for in it—in short, a program for reading.

But often the hearer or reader must guess how to listen or read on the basis of clues embedded in the communication itself, clues that tip off the hearers or readers that the communicator has moved into a particular type of communication. "Once upon a time" signals *fairy tale*; "Dear Angela," at the top of the page cues a *letter*. "Did ya' hear the one about the two sailors and the parrot?" lets the hearers know they are in for a *joke*. Sometimes these clues are quite subtle, of course, and sometimes they are even intentionally concealed for a moment. A joke, for example, may be presented as straightforward communication until the punch line. The punch line, however, is an unmistakable though belated tip-off that we have been participating in a joke all along, and the hearing of the punch line causes us to reassess the previous details of the joke in this new light.

In many cases there are also unstated but nonetheless discernible clues to be found in the context of the communication. If a woman walks over to us at a party, extends her hand, and says, "I'm Susan Kim," we instantly know that we are to shake her hand and respond

with our own name. We know this not only because she has stated
her name but because the circumstances around her words tell us that
in this instance her giving her name is part of a formalized pattern of
communication which can be called "the social introduction." Now,
suppose our speaker had walked to the lectern of the annual meeting
of the Academy of Science, arranged her lecture notes, adjusted the
microphone, and then said to the audience of several hundred people,
"I'm Susan Kim." It would be a surprise, not to mention a serious
misunderstanding of the nature of the moment, if someone in the
crowd were to pop up to respond, "Hello Susan, I'm Robert Ludkin."
Just as the syntax of a sentence forms a mutually agreed-upon pattern
of communication, social convention provides the framework into
which the bits and pieces of communication may be organized into a
meaningful whole.

Contextual clues appear in written as well as in oral communication. Many years ago Bliss Perry, in A Study of Poetry, commented on
the following sentence which appeared in a physics textbook: "And
hence no force, however great, can draw a cord, however fine, into a
horizontal line which shall be absolutely straight." Perry noted that
this sentence, arranged into verse form, has a Tennyson-like rhyme
and meter scheme.[4]

And hence no force, however great,
   Can draw a cord, however fine,
   Into a horizontal line
Which shall be absolutely straight.

These twenty-one words, simply placed one after the other, can
be read as either physics or poetry. If they are physics, we take them
at face value, as a statement of scientific fact. If they are poetry, our
minds go galloping after metaphor, symbolism, and other poetic
devices. What guides us toward the former understanding is the
placement of the words within the context of a textbook entitled
The Parallelogram of Forces. This does not eliminate the possibility
that the author is being clever and slipping a little poetry in with the
matter-of-fact prose, but if that were the case there would be at least
one clue to the reader somewhere. Otherwise, it could only be the
author's private joke.

FOLLOWING THE PARTNER'S LEAD

We can now draw together the threads of this discussion about human communication. Since biblical texts, that is, written communication, will be our concern from this point on, we must concentrate upon the text-reader relationship.

The general picture looks like this: An experienced reader comes to a text with a storehouse of skills and aptitudes and a repertoire of reading strategies acquired through previous encounters with various forms of literature. When a reader encounters a particular text, he or she attempts to get on common ground with the text by guessing, on the basis of clues in the text and context, which of the reading strategies is appropriate, expecting to play this game by these rules rather than some other. If as the reading process unfolds the guess proves wrong, the reader guesses again on the basis of additional clues until there is, if possible, a "fit" between the form and dynamics of the text and the strategy employed by the reader.

When there is a relative degree of cooperation between text and reader, communication occurs—the text does something with and to the reader. The cooperation necessary for this to happen does not mean that the reader can predict everything that will take place in the text. There are surprises, but the surprises gain their power by virtue of taking place within the reasonably stable framework of forms shared by author and reader.

This reading process is, of course, largely an unconscious activity. Most of the time we do not have to think about it at all; we just do it. But shifting this activity as it applies to biblical texts into the conscious arena will allow us to identify and be attentive to the ways biblical texts invite us to read and therefore to experience them in psalmic, parabolic, narrative, and other ways.

Wolfgang Iser, a noted student of the dynamics of reading, has stated, "If communication between text and reader is to be successful, clearly the reader's activity must . . . be controlled in some way by the text."[5] My goals here are to seek the sources of that control in biblical texts and to determine how preachers can be guided by that control in sermons.

It is fully possible, of course, for the control to run in the opposite direction. Because we come to texts not as blank tablets but armed with expectations, we already have an investment in how a text should read. That prior expectation exerts a powerful influence over the communication process. While this influence cannot entirely be overcome, it can be disciplined by a willingness to allow the text to take the dominant role in guiding communication. Without this willingness, there is nothing to guarantee that the text will be heard. If I choose, for example, to read a letter of rejection as a love letter in disguise, the chances are better than good that I can force the reading process to come out my way. Texts are limited in their ability to fight back.

Our task now is to discover how these insights about human communication apply to the very particular process of moving from a biblical text to a sermon, and we turn our attention to that in chapter 2.

2
MOVING
from text to sermon

READING A TEXT—PREACHING A TEXT

I described in chapter 1 some of the dynamics that can occur in the interaction between a text and a reader. What implications does this understanding of the reading process have for the exegesis of biblical texts, especially that exegesis which is headed toward the eventual goal of preaching? A recent volume on biblical exegesis indicates that "one way to think about the exegetical task is to conceive of it as learning to interrogate the biblical text."[1] If this is so, an understanding of the communicational aspects of reading texts would suggest that the usual set of questions brought by the preacher to a text must be expanded. In addition to such traditional exegetical questions as authorship, date, and occasion, we must ask questions aimed at discovering the literary dynamics of the text, how the text guides the reading process, and what rhetorical effects may be created in the reader by the text.

Most seminary-trained ministers have been schooled to analyze biblical texts as documents which were shaped by the circumstances in which they originated, and thus they ask historical questions of those texts. One of the enduring contributions of the historical-critical approach to Scripture has been the recognition that biblical passages do not spring from thin air. They are not expressions of disembodied and timeless truths or "messages from heaven" disconnected from concrete historical circumstances. Biblical texts were written by particular people employing particular resources in particular circumstances and for particular purposes. In short, biblical texts have a *history*, and

the methods of historical-critical research have proved fruitful in un-
covering that history. Preachers have learned to interrogate scriptural
texts by asking such historical questions as, Who wrote this? To
Whom? When? Why?

This style of historical inquiry has sometimes been pictured as an
investigation *behind* the text. What is the text's past? Where did it
come from? What did it once "mean" in a particular time and place?
These historical questions and concerns need not be abandoned.
Instead, they should be augmented by questions that lead to a close
analysis of the literary features *in* the texts and the rhetorical dynamics which are likely to take place *in front of* the texts, that is, *between*
text and reader. To ask such questions both does and does not move
beyond traditional historical criticism. There is a long list of questions that could be asked about the literary and rhetorical aspects of
texts, but the following questions provide a focus to our approach:

1. What is the genre of the text?
2. What is the rhetorical function of this genre?
3. What literary devices does this genre employ to achieve its
   rhetorical effect?
4. How in particular does the text under consideration, in its own
   literary setting, embody the characteristics and dynamics described in questions 1–3?

To these exegetical questions we can add a homiletical question:

5. How may the sermon, in a new setting, say and do what the text
   says and does in its setting?

INTERROGATING THE TEXT

Let us now consider each of the key questions.

1. *What is the genre of the text?*

Biblical scholar John Barton has defined the term *genre* as "a conventional pattern, recognizable by certain formal criteria (style, shape,
tone, particular syntactic or even grammatical structures, recurring
formulaic patterns), which is used in a particular society in social contexts which are governed by certain formal conventions."[2]

That is a tightly packed statement, and in order to see how this
definition could apply to a particular case, consider the following
poem.

There was a young woman named Bright,
Whose speed was much faster than light.
She set out one day
In a relative way
And returned on the previous night.[3]

We quickly recognize this, of course, as a *limerick.* It is important to notice that as soon as we have said, "That's a limerick," we have named its genre. How did we recognize that? The answer, of course, is that even though no two limericks are identical, all limericks are alike in some important ways, and this poem fits a general scheme common to limericks. Because it exhibits the mainly anapestic meter, the requisite five lines, the rhyme scheme *aabba,* and the humorous subject matter typical of limericks, we easily recognize it as a limerick. To use Barton's terminology, a limerick is a genre because it is "a conventional pattern, recognizable by certain formal criteria." This poem is identified as a limerick because it fits the conventional limerick pattern.

Not all societies, however, have limericks. We can find limericks on the restroom walls of nearly every American high school, but we would have searched in vain for one in ancient Babylon. Cultures create their own genres or patterns that, in Barton's words, are "used in a particular society in social contexts which are governed by certain formal conventions." Some genres, the advertising jingle, for example, are very culture specific. Others, such as folk narratives, are virtually universal. Still others, such as epistles, are present in some form in almost every society but vary significantly in pattern from culture to culture.

The Bible includes many genres: psalms, proverbs, miracle stories, parables, prophetic oracles, and short stories, to name but a few. All of these genres embody characteristic literary patterns common to the literature of the cultures in which the Bible arose. First, then, we must identify the particular pattern present in a text by naming its genre.

2. What is the rhetorical function of this genre?

Once we have identified the genre of a text, the next question becomes, What is this particular genre designed to *do* in the reading process? It is important to distinguish at this point between the literary features of a text and its rhetorical function or dynamics. The literary features are those elements of language and sequence that make the text what it is. The rhetorical dynamics are the effects that the literary features are intended to produce in a reader. Literary features are in the text; rhetorical dynamics, though caused by the text, are in the reader. A punch line is a literary feature of a written joke; the laughter caused by the punch line is a rhetorical dynamic.

This question, then, tries to discover what effect the genre of a text is likely to have on a typical reader or hearer. Sometimes this is fairly easy to determine. A *joke* is a genre designed to make us laugh. A *riddle* is a genre designed to make us think in certain oblique ways. A *ghost story* is a genre designed to frighten us.

Much of the time, however, genres have more complex and multi-layered rhetorical functions. It is not easy to say what a parable or a psalm or a proverb is likely to do for and to a reader, and any attempt to describe the rhetorical dynamics of such genres will be found wanting. Nevertheless, each genre does possess specific rhetorical impact. A parable does something to a reader that a psalm does not do, and vice versa. In our quest to understand the possible meanings of each of these types of genre, we must be prepared to say what we can about the rhetorical dynamics. We cannot know everything, but what we do know is important.

Asking about the rhetorical dynamics that may take place within a reader may appear tantamount to abandoning the stability of the text itself in favor of the uncertainty of the interior life of the reader and, thereby, entering into a swamp of hopeless subjectivity. What a text "does" to one reader may be quite different from what that same text does to another. Where does the control over the interpretive process lie?

In order to respond to this question, it is crucial to reaffirm that we are building here on the understanding of the reading process described in chapter 1. Reading was described there as an active process involving the interaction between the reader's informed expectations and the text itself. Texts, it is important to remember, have the capacity to exercise powerful guiding influence over the willing and careful reader. While it is true that meaning occurs within a reader and that what a reader brings to the interaction both limits and contributes to that meaning, for an attentive reader the meaning is controlled by the content and the literary dynamics of the text itself.

Not everyone agrees, of course, with this understanding of the interaction between text and reader. The literary critic Stanley Fish, for example, is persuaded that meanings exist in neither texts nor readers but rather in the "interpretive communities" to which readers belong. Fish does not explain precisely what he means by an interpretive community, but he seems to mean a group that shares the same values, purposes, and goals. A political caucus or a theological party would apparently count as an interpretive community. In any case, he does say that "it is interpretive communities, rather than either the text or the reader, that produce meanings and are responsible for the emergence of formal features."[4]

As an illustration, Fish cites an event which occurred one day in his class. He was teaching two courses in the same classroom. The first class, held at 9:30 in the morning, was considering the relationship between linguistics and literary criticism. At 11:00 o'clock, this first group was replaced by another set of students who were studying seventeenth-century English religious poetry. In Fish's terminology, the two classes formed different interpretive communities.

Fish wrote on the blackboard an assignment for the first class, a list of the last names of certain linguists and literary critics whose works were to be studied by the class. It read:

Jacobs-Rosenbaum
Levin
Thorne
Hayes
Ohman (?)

Ohmann's name was followed by a question mark because Fish was, at the moment, uncertain about whether it was spelled with one or two n's.

Before the second class arrived, Fish, as an experiment, drew a frame around the list and wrote "p. 43" at the top of the frame. He told the second group of students that what they saw on the board was a religious poem of the kind they had been studying and asked them to interpret it. The results were both highly creative and to Fish's way of thinking entirely predictable. The students found all manner of religious content in the list: Jacobs was seen as a reference to Jacob's ladder. Rosenbaum was a "rose tree," thus the Virgin Mary, a rose

without thorns. Thorne was an allusion to Jesus' crown of thorns.
Ohman was "oh man." Even the graphic shape the words formed was
construed as a symbol for a cross or an altar. Fish wrote,

> As soon as my students were aware that it was poetry they were seeing,
> they began to look with poetry-seeing eyes, that is, with eyes that saw
> everything in relation to the properties they knew poems to pos-
> sess. . . . Thus the meanings of the words and the interpretation in
> which those words were seen to be embedded emerged together, as a
> consequence of the operations my students began to perform once
> they were told that this was a poem.
>
> It was almost as if they were following a recipe—if it's a poem do
> this, if it's a poem, see it that way—and indeed definitions of poetry
> *are* recipes, for by directing readers as to what to look for in a poem,
> they instruct them in ways of looking which will produce what they
> expect to see. . . . Skilled reading is usually thought to be a matter
> of discerning what is there, but if the example of my students can be
> generalized, it is a matter of knowing how to *produce* what can there-
> after be said to be there. Interpretation is not the art of construing but
> the art of constructing. Interpreters do not decode poems; they make
> them.[5]

Fish's point, of course, is that since his class on religious poetry was
an interpretive community it operated as just such a community, using
the text on the board as an occasion for bringing forth the meanings
already present in the group under the guise of discerning meanings in
the text. Indeed, there are no meanings as such *in* the text.

Fish's argument cannot be lightly dismissed in biblical interpretation. Indeed, there are countless examples in the history of interpretation (negative examples, I would argue) that lend support to his case.
Fundamentalists, charismatics, social activists, feminists, evangelicals,
traditionalists, liberationists—all of us, in fact—go to the texts of the
Bible and return with trophies that are replicas of our own theological
image. It is no easy task genuinely to listen to the voice of Scripture
rather than merely to hear the sound of our own echoes.

Moreover, there is an aspect of the concept of interpretive communities that has a positive value in biblical interpretation. An
interpreter who lives and moves within the community of faith
goes to the Bible assuming that its texts will speak in a way that
other documents do not. However one defines the doctrinal notion
of the authority of Scripture, the conviction that Scripture has a

distinctive claim upon us is common to virtually all theological positions. Once we know that a certain text is biblical, we put into play expectations different from those we would have were we interpreting another kind of text.

Fish apparently would claim (and there is irony in the very attempt to understand what his book is saying) that the expectations that originate in the interpretive community fully control the interpretive process. In Fish's view, we go to texts like Scripture not to find meaning but to make it. In contrast, I maintain that encounters with Scripture itself have built up in the community of faith the expectation of Scripture's special character, rather than the other way around. The expectations a faithful interpreter brings to Scripture are not imposed upon those documents entirely from without but are derived from the history of the community's previous engagement with the Bible.

The literary critic Robert Scholes disputes the "proof" of Fish's classroom case, saying,

> Suppose that what had been left on the blackboard was not simply a list of names in a vaguely emblematic shape. Suppose the text had taken the form of a prose statement of the assignment that read as follows:
>
> For next Thursday read the essays in the Jacobs and Rosenbaum anthology by Levin, Thorne, Hayes, and Ohmann.
>
> If this were the case, would Fish have told the class that the text constituted a religious poem? If he had, would they have succeeded so splendidly in perceiving it as one? I think the answer to both questions is, "No." To any competent reader of English the prosaic quality of this sentence would make it difficult to perceive as poetry. I'm not saying it couldn't be done. I am saying it wouldn't be done.[6]

Scholes argues that the text itself contains signals, clues, and codes which control to a high degree the process of reading. In summarizing his case, he ably states a crucial point of this book as well: "Texts have a certain reality. A change in a letter or a mark of punctuation can force us to perceive them differently, read them differently, and interpret them differently."[7]

Texts have a certain reality. This is the crucial point. In a variety of ways the reality of biblical texts has signaled to the community of faith those texts' special status as Scripture. Now they signal to the careful reader how they are to be read. Thus the texts themselves govern the rhetorical possibilities.

3. What literary devices does this genre employ to achieve its rhetorical effect?

The previous question asked what the text *does* for and to the reader. This question asks, *How* does the text do what it does? What literary features are present in the text which allow it to accomplish its rhetorical work?

Suppose we are dealing with the genre of *pun*. A sports announcer recently spoke this example: "The reason San Francisco's baseball stadium, Candlestick Park, is so chilly is because there are so many Giant fans there." Typical of a pun, this was designed to produce a giggle or a groan, more likely the latter. But how does it achieve this effect? Obviously through a play on the words "Giant fans," which in the context of the pun, can mean either of two different things, both of which the pun calls for us to hold in tension at once. The pun does its rhetorical work through this double meaning.

Every literary genre has characteristic literary features through which it does its work and achieves its effect in the reader or hearer. This step in the analytical process calls for us to dissect the particular genre and isolate the elements by which this genre produces its impact.

4. How in particular does the text under consideration, in its own literary setting, embody the characteristics and dynamics described in the previous questions?

In the first three questions we have asked how a text fits into a broad category of genre, and we have therefore focused upon the continuities between one text and the many other texts of the same type. With this question, we turn to the peculiarities of a particular text to see how *this* text, while fitting the pattern of its genre, is nonetheless unique. Suppose, for example, the text under consideration were Matt. 1:1–17. In answer to the first question, we would identify this as an example of the *genealogy* genre. Indeed, the first verse actually names the genre for the reader.

The second question calls upon us to ponder the rhetorical effects of the particular genre. What *happens* to a reader when encountering a genealogy? What expectations are triggered by this genre and put into play in the reading process? One obvious response is that the reader gains a broader and deeper sense of the identity of the person whose genealogy is given. People are born into families and shaped by them; so, through a genealogy, the reader gets to "know" the person in a richer and more complex way. Genealogies also have to do with status. A genealogy is in part a social pedigree aimed at providing credentials for a person; the reader is invited to make judgments about a person's social rank by seeing that person in the context of his or her lineage.

Moreover, any names in the genealogy that the reader might recognize evoke memories and associations connected to those names. To a sophomore in a high school literature class, learning that Harriet Beecher Stowe wrote *Uncle Tom's Cabin* may represent only another name to memorize. To a student of American history, though, learning that Harriet was the daughter of Lyman Beecher—not to mention the sister of Henry Ward Beecher—not only enriches the student's understanding of Stowe's social and intellectual identity but also evokes all that the student knows about her famous and controversial clergyman father.

The third question invites us to identify the literary dynamics of the genre that allow it to achieve its rhetorical effects. A genealogy accomplishes its work not merely by listing names but also by providing those names in chronological order and by linking them through the fact of paternity. It has been suggested that the telephone directory would become far more interesting if each listing were followed by the word "begat." We would then have, not a tedious list of names, but a network of relationships with endlessly fascinating linkages.

In response to the fourth question, when we turn to the Matthean genealogy of Jesus in particular, we find that the dynamics of the genre are in place—a chronological listing of names, and the phrase "the father of" joining one name to the next. Many of these names are familiar—Abraham, Boaz, David, Solomon—and evoke memories of stories.

But there are some surprises in the text too. First, Matthew pauses along the way to guide our memory by pointing out various facts: for instance, that David was "the king" and that Jechoniah had brothers and lived "at the time of the deportation to Babylon." Almost all genealogies evoke memories of persons and events, but not all genealogies suspend the marching list of names in order to aim the remembering process. Matthew's does, and it is a small but significant departure from the norm. A second surprise is that Matthew groups the names into three sets of fourteen: Abraham to David, David to the exile, and the exile to Jesus (v. 17). This is not standard genealogical practice, and we are left to wonder about the purpose of this symmetry.

Yet another surprise is the appearance of women's names. Judah, we are told, was the father of Perez and Zerah "by Tamar"; Salmon was the father of Boaz "by Rahab"; and Boaz was the father of Obed "by Ruth." The phrase, "David was the father of Solomon by the wife of Uriah," implies the presence of Bathsheba and reminds us of David's sinful liaison. These references prepare us, in a way, for the biggest surprise of all—the presence of the name of Mary in the very lineal progress of the genealogy: "Jacob the father of Joseph the husband of Mary, of whom Jesus was born." Thus the genealogical formula is both fulfilled and, in a startling manner, broken.

What a close reading of Matthew's genealogy reveals is typical in its particularity of what emerges in the encounter with almost every text. This text *largely* fits the pattern of the genealogical genre, and because of that a reader knows what to expect from the text and puts those expectations into play in the reading process. But notice what the text does with and to those expectations. In some places, it simply confirms them. The reader finds what was expected, and the reading proceeds in a relatively comfortable and conventional way. In other places, however, while the text fulfills the expectations, it does so in an unusual and nuanced fashion. A ripple of uncertainty interrupts the reading process, causing the reader to pause and ponder. In still other places, the text violates the reader's expectations and thereby has a new and unanticipated rhetorical impact on the reader.

These observations, when applied to the Matthean genealogy, have much import in terms of interpreting the text. Jesus, for example, is given a pedigree in which his name evokes not only a connection with royalty but also memories of the full sweep of Israel's history. The emphasis upon Abraham and David and the explicit references to the exile and to David as "the king" emphasize this identity and underscore these historic memories. The threefold grouping of the list into sets of fourteen gives a sense of overall design. An impression is created for the reader that this unfolding of the numberless generations is not random but proceeds according to an overarching plan that is purposeful from beginning to end. The unusual presence of the women in the list works to trouble or unsettle the reader with the knowledge that this overall design does not take the form of a straight path; there were twists and detours along the genealogical road from Abraham to Jesus. Moreover, the writer of Matthew has chosen to *begin* the Gospel with this genealogy. In sum, its rhetorical effect is to say, "Let me introduce you to Jesus the Christ, the one who, by the design of God, is the inheritor of David's kingship and the fullness of Israel's history, but in ways which will surprise and trouble you. Listen now to his story. . . ."

5. How may the sermon, in a new setting, say and do what the text says and does in its setting?

This final question, homiletical in nature, seeks to find an explicit connection between the text and the sermon. We have seen how biblical texts through the interlacing of content and literary form both say and do things in the reading process. The sermon's task is to extend a portion of the text's impact into a new communicational situation, that of contemporary hearers listening to the sermon. I say a portion of the text's impact because no sermon can exhaust the possibilities for meaning present in a biblical text.

There are two possible misconceptions of this step which must be addressed. First, since the text achieves its rhetorical impact through its particular literary form, it may seem that the preacher who wishes to be faithful to the text has no choice but to select the same literary form for the sermon. In other words, a sermon on a narrative text would be a narrative itself, a sermon on a psalm would be a poem. This would obviously be both difficult and impractical.

The preacher's task, though, is not to replicate the text but to regenerate the impact of some portion of that text. He or she must not attempt to say and do everything the text once said and did. Rather the preacher should attempt to say and do what a *portion* of the text *now* says and does for a new and unique set of people. Moreover, the preacher does this in the oral sermonic form, which is itself a genre with accompanying expectations and conventions. This means that the preacher always faces a critical communicational question regarding the sermon, How can I shape the sermon to achieve for the contemporary hearer what some aspect of the text wishes to achieve? While the literary form of the text may at times serve as a model for the form of the sermon, on other occasions the preacher, in order to be faithful to the text, will select for the sermon a markedly different pattern.

A second misconception involves the notion that traveling from text to sermon involves a series of unilateral moves: *from* determining the meaning of the text *to* deciding how to apply that meaning to the contemporary situation in the sermon. This description overlooks the middle term of interpretation—the fact that the contemporary situation, including the theological convictions of the community, is already present, through the interpreter, in the activity of textual interpretation.

While it is true that the biblical text assumes a dominant role in the process of interpretation, meaning erupts in the interaction between text and interpreter. The text controls the process of reading, but what the reader brings to that encounter imposes limits upon and creates possibilities for that process. Because the text exerts control, there are boundaries beyond which interpretation may not go and still claim textual validity. But because each time a text is read the circumstances of reading are different, new meanings are always emerging. Preaching does not involve determining what the text used to mean and then devising some creative way to make that meaning pertinent to the contemporary scene. Preaching involves a contemporary interpreter closely attending to a text, discerning the claim that text makes upon the current life of the community of faith, and announcing that discovery in the sermon.

THE READING OF TEXTS AND
HISTORICAL CRITICISM

How does this approach to biblical texts relate to the more traditional methods of historical-critical analysis? In the main, literary-rhetorical concerns simply add to the repertoire of questions asked of the text by the careful interpreter. They provide another angle of vision from which to view the text.

There is at least one practical way, however, in which this approach redirects the energies of the historical critic: historical tools may be applied to reconstruct the "original rhetorical situation." In other words, given the fact that literary genres are socially and historically conditioned, we are concerned to know what the original readers would have expected of a particular text and how the text may have affected them.

This carries us into a complex issue in modern hermeneutics. Contemporary theories of interpretation make an important distinction between spoken and written communication. If someone says to us, "Do not let the sun go down on your anger," and we do not know what the person is trying to say, we can ask, "What do you mean by that?" The speaker can then clarify his or her intention. But if we run across the same phrase in written form, as we do in Eph. 4:26, we have only the text since the author is not around to clarify what was intended. We are left with the text and the text alone.

While this may seem to be a disadvantage for written communication, contemporary hermeneutical theory does not see it that way. To the contrary, to put something in writing is to set it free from the particular set of circumstances that were present at the time of its writing and to invite other readers in other circumstances to find new meaning there. According to Paul Ricoeur,

> [Writing] renders the text autonomous with respect to the intention of the author. What the text signifies no longer coincides with what the author meant; henceforth, textual meaning and psychological meaning have different destinies. . . .
>
> What is true of the psychological conditions holds also for the sociological conditions of the production of the work. An essential characteristic of a literary work, and of a work of art in general, is that it transcends its own psycho-sociological conditions of production and thereby opens itself to an unlimited series of readings, themselves situated in different socio-cultural situations. In short, the text must be able, from the sociological as well as from the psychological point of view, to "decontextualize" itself in such a way that it can be "recontextualized" in a new situation—as accomplished, precisely, by the act of reading.[8]

Oral communication, in other words, grows out of a concrete situation and possesses meaning in relation to its setting. When asked, our speaker may respond, "When I said, 'Don't let the sun go down on your anger,' I meant that I think you should not stew about it, but should go right now and tell your friend you're upset that he forgot your lunch appointment." That and nothing else is what our speaker's statement meant because oral communication is limited to the intention of the speaker and to the common situation of speaker and hearer.

Written communication, on the other hand, because it is fixed in writing transcends the circumstances surrounding its creation. The author is no longer present, and the reader and the author do not share a common situation. Unlike the spoken word, a written text is sent hurtling through time and space and is free to interact with ever new and different situations. When we read, "Don't let the sun go down on your anger," we seek to discover what possibilities the text opens up for us, even though our circumstances are quite different from those present when the text was written. Oral statements have situations; texts have "worlds."

This may sound like license to ignore historical factors about texts in favor of the immediate response upon reading them anew, but that is not the case. The irony is that we must gain as much historical information about a text as possible precisely in order to free it to speak to a new situation. The King James Version (KJV) of the Bible, for example, uses the word "prevent" to say what is meant today by the phrase "go before." The KJV translates a line in Ps. 79:8 as, "Let thy tender mercies speedily prevent us." The RSV translation reads, "Let thy compassion come speedily to meet us." The interpreter using the KJV, then, needs to know the seventeenth-century historical connotation of the term precisely in order to hear rather than mishear the text in its new situation. The same is true regarding historical information concerning literary and rhetorical matters.

In order to see how the literary and rhetorical approach to interpreting texts depends upon historical research and yet redirects those efforts, let us consider Phil. 2:5-11. There is no lack of rich historical and theological commentary available on this text. Its fate in the hands of commentators concerned with traditional historical-critical issues, but not rhetorical issues, is exemplified in Kenneth Grayston's comments.[9] His brief treatment of this passage is an able, clear, and fairly typical example of the traditional approach:

1. Grayston begins by noting that in Greek vv. 6-11 are poetic in character, suggesting that this portion of the passage may be a hymn. He even tries to arrange the passage into stanzas.

2. He then notes that the words and thoughts of this hymnic portion are not those typically found elsewhere in Paul, which could indicate that Paul is quoting an already existing hymn. If so, "then presumably its original setting was the church's worship" (p. 22).

3. Next he rehearses the scholarly debate concerning whether the mythic and theological themes in the hymn originated in Jewish, Hellenistic, or Persian thought.

4. Finally, after stating that the hymn in not intended to be a formal christological statement, but is more like the liturgical hymns found in Revelation, he performs a verse-by-verse linguistic, historical, and theological analysis of the passage.

Now, notice what is happening here. From a rhetorical perspective, Grayston is like a detective who has all the evidence but cannot yet see how the clues fit the case. He knows or at least suspects that Paul, in the middle of a letter to the Philippian church, interrupted the flow of his epistolary prose for a few lines of hymn singing. Moreover, he speculates that the immediate source of the hymn was "the Church's worship," and he recognizes that this piece of poetry in Philippians is more like the liturgical singing found in Revelation than like systematic theology.

It appears that the Philippian Christians reading this letter suddenly encountered a passage in which their beloved teacher Paul burst into song, perhaps even one of *their* Sunday hymns. If this is the case, this is more than just interesting historical data: it is crucial to the interpretation of the text. To use the terms of chapter 1, letters and hymns are discrete literary forms that trigger different expectations and demand different reading strategies. A hymn does something to the reader which other literary forms do not do, so Paul's choice of a hymn at this juncture in the letter is artful, not accidental. The effect upon the reader is distinctive, and that effect is a part of the meaning of the passage.

Grayston, however, promptly tosses aside his discovery in favor of a detailed—albeit skillful—analysis of the historical and theological issues in each of the verses which, while necessary and helpful, misses the rhetorical point. The idea that Paul quoted a liturgical hymn is, for Grayston, historically interesting, but hermeneutically irrelevant. It tells us something about where the text came from and how it may have been used before Paul put it in his letter, but almost nothing about its meaning then or now. To be fair, Grayston's commentary and others like it do not speak to this issue because the methodology employed does not systematically raise the rhetorical question. Homiletics, however, cannot avoid the question.

Examining this text from the literary-rhetorical perspective outlined here involves taking the findings of the sort of exegesis Grayston does, but employing them in a different way. We note, for example, that this passage appears as a part of the epistle genre: Paul quotes a liturgical hymn in the middle of a letter written to people with whom he has an established pastoral relationship. To imagine the impact Paul's letter might have had, picture a university student, away from home and struggling with personal and academic problems, going to his campus mailbox and finding there a handwritten letter from his pastor. The pastor writes:

> And so, I want you to know that you are always in my prayers, but more important than that, you are under God's protection and care. Grant us wisdom, grant us courage, for the living of these days, for the living of these days.

Here, as in Philippians, a pastor quotes a hymn in the midst of a letter (Harry Emerson Fosdick's "God of Grace and God of Glory"). What would be the effect upon the student? We cannot know for sure, but we can venture a guess: the student knows this hymn and has sung it many times. The lines from the hymn evoke the ethos of his home congregation at worship. They bring into his active memory the sound of his own voice singing that hymn with others, perhaps even some particular occasions when it was sung. This memory and the very words of the hymn introduce a measure of calm, stability, and patient faithfulness into the student's uncertainty. In short, the quotation creates an effect and thereby produces a total meaning which would not be as complete if the pastor had instead written, "Pray that God will give you the wisdom to endure through your struggles."

Now if we were trying to interpret this letter using Grayston's method, we would ignore all of that and focus instead on an analysis of the language and theology of Fosdick's hymn itself. This approach would not be entirely off the mark, of course, but it would not hit the hermeneutical nail on the head unless it moved on to the question of how that theology worked through the hymnic literary form to create meaning for the reader.

Some may object, of course, that the sort of textual reading I suggest is too speculative to be reliable. What if the Philippians *do not* already know the hymn Paul is quoting? Or what if Paul is not quoting at all, but composed the poem on the spot, or inserted Christian language into a snippet of Persian verse he happened to have up his educated sleeve? Two responses may be made.

1. The objection simply demonstrates how a literary and rhetorical approach to Scripture must work in tandem with the more traditional historical approach. If the historical data point toward a liturgical origin for the hymn, that is rhetorically significant. If the evidence points in the other direction or is ambiguous, that is rhetorically significant also. The relationship between literary criticism and historical criticism is important and will be addressed in more detail later.

2. The literary approach, it may be argued, is less speculative than a purely historical investigation because we actually have the text in hand. Whatever the historical origins of Phil. 2:5-11 may be, the fact is we have before us an epistolary form with a hymnic form in its midst. How this blending of forms would affect readers is open for debate but that debate will always return to what is clearly *known* — the literary shape of the text. As Robert Alter commented,

> [Since literary] features are linked to discernible details in the . . . text, the literary approach is actually a good deal *less* conjectural than the historical scholarship which asks of a verse whether it contains possible Akkadian loanwords, whether it reflects Sumerian kinship practices, whether it may have been corrupted by scribal error.[10]

Our task now is to see how this approach to biblical preaching works in relation to particular biblical genres, such as narrative, prophetic oracle, proverb, psalm, parable, and epistle.

3
PREACHING
on the psalms

Even today when public knowledge of the Bible is at a low ebb, the psalms maintain their grip upon the popular memory and imagination. "The Lord is my shepherd, I shall not want"; "Lord, thou hast been our dwelling place in all generations"; "Make a joyful noise to the Lord"; "Bless the Lord, O my soul; and all that is within me, bless his holy name!" "Let everything that breathes praise the Lord." These phrases are not only in the general cultural repertoire, they also stimulate personal memories of countless funerals and baccalaureates, weddings and homecomings, occasions of great joy and moments of deep sadness.

Although the psalms are among the best known and most loved texts of Scripture, there are preachers who refuse on principle to preach sermons based upon psalms. They refuse not because they are stubborn, dislike the psalms, or fail to find profound meaning in them. Instead, they see the psalms as songs to be sung rather than as sermon texts to be preached, prayerful praise and laments more appropriately found on the lips of the congregation rather than instructional texts exposited by the preacher. To these preachers, preaching on a psalm would be like preaching on Michelangelo's *David* —too much would be lost in the translation.

There is no good reason, though, why the psalms cannot be sung *and* preached. In the same way that the Apostles' Creed, normally a liturgical confessional statement, at times becomes the focus of a series of doctrinal sermons, the rich theological texture of the psalms justifies their liturgical use as sermon texts as well as musical texts. To do so enables singing and preaching to become mutually reinforcing activities in worship.

The hesitancy of some to preach on a psalm, however, indirectly makes one of the key points of this book. The reluctance to employ a literary form intended for one purpose as the basis for another activity (here, musical prayer as the basis for preaching) indicates both a recognition that psalms possess special literary and functional qualities and a respect for those qualities. The challenge before us is to approach preaching on psalm texts in a way that respects their unique literary characteristics. To do so, we must examine the genre psalms by asking the questions developed in chapter 2.

What is the genre of the text?

Psalms are poetic liturgical prayers. This means, first, that psalms are poetry, Hebrew poetry to be specific, and that they obey the conventions of that literary form. It also means that the psalms are poems which eventually came to be sung, chanted, or recited over and over again in worship, and thus were stylized to fit into the liturgical context. This does not mean that all psalms were originally composed as liturgical texts. Indeed, the *Sitz im Leben* of individual psalms has been a matter of debate in contemporary scholarship. Cultic ceremonies, juridical procedures, personal prayer, and domestic rituals have all been suggested as the sources for various psalms. Whatever the circumstances surrounding the birth of a given psalm, though, every psalm in the psalter eventually came to be a part of the collection of psalms that, as Patrick D. Miller, Jr., states, "have functioned in the *worship* of the community of faith, Jewish and Christian, widely, extensively, and without break."[1]

Although Claus Westermann and other students of the psalms warn against the easy use of this analogy,[2] the psalms are nonetheless much like the texts of modern hymns. They are poems, and they more or less obey the "rules" of poetry; but they are poems which also bear the marks and carry the memories of their repeated use in worship.

What is the rhetorical function of this genre?

Because psalms are poems, they do what poems do—not an easy thing to describe. Laurence Perrine attempted indirectly to characterize poetic action, when he warned his students not to read poetry while lying in a hammock because poetry's "purpose is not to soothe and relax, but to arouse and awake, to shock into life, to make one more alive."[3] Other forms of imaginative literature, such as novels and plays, seek the same ends, Perrine acknowledged, but the difference between them and poetry "is one of degree." Poetry, he claimed, is more "condensed and concentrated," has a "higher voltage" than other literary forms, and applies "greater pressure per word."[4]

All of this talk of higher voltage and word pressure points to the fact that poetry works to disrupt the customary ways in which we use language. Poetry stretches the ordinary uses of words, and places them into unfamiliar relationships with each other, thereby cutting fresh paths across the well-worn grooves of everyday language. Poems change what we think and feel not by piling up facts we did not know or by persuading us through arguments, but by making finely tuned adjustments at deep and critical places in our imaginations.

For example, when the psalmist says,

As a hart longs
   for flowing streams,
so longs my soul
   for thee, O God.
      (Ps. 42:1)

the words penetrate directly to that place where we visualize our primary relationship to God. They go behind theological propositions regarding divine-human interaction to the source symbols from which those affirmations spring. Perrine's "high voltage" description is apt because an alteration of theological vision at this level can cause an entire theological world view to spring forth or fall apart.

As I noted earlier, psalms are not only poems, to be read and interpreted as just poems. They are poems which came to have repeated liturgical usage. Walter Brueggemann has suggested a threefold use of the psalms common to both ancient Israel and the modern church: liturgical, devotional, and pastoral.[5] While it is true that the psalms have functioned in each of these ways, I suggest that their primary function has always been liturgical, both logically and hermeneutically. That psalms have been used in personal devotion and in pastoral care to a greater extent than have other biblical genres is due not only to their intrinsic experiential qualities but also to the

memories associated with them built up through their frequent repetition in corporate worship.

This fact of the psalms' liturgical character modifies and sharpens
what we can say about their rhetorical impact beyond that discerned
through the realization that the psalms are poetry. It is one thing to
read a poem with a religious theme, say, Tennyson's "Flower in the
Crannied Wall." It is another to encounter a poem with a religious
theme which has been used over and over in worship, Tennyson's
"Strong Son of God, Immortal Love," for instance, which has been
set to music, been employed as a Christian hymn, and become a
possession of the whole community of faith. It has gained its strength
through its "fit" with the church's established patterns of religious
experience in a way not possible by "Flower in a Crannied Wall."

When we read Psalm 23 at a funeral, for example, there is something
new about the experience: it is *this* funeral, *this* unique death, *this*
special grief, *this* unrepeatable moment which is being brought *this* day
to the psalm. But there is something old and familiar at work as well.
The grooves of this psalm are well-worn, its rhythms sure and com-
forting. Part of hearing the psalm involves the realization that we have
been this way many times before, and the uncommonness of this occasion is gathered into the constancy of the psalm. We hope and trust
that this psalm will do again what it has done on countless previous
occasions.

This is true even of those psalms which are by no means reassuring
in theme and force, psalms of lament and anguish, those psalms
Walter Brueggemann terms "psalms of dislocation."[6] The fact that
the Psalter contains psalms of anger, abandonment, and despair af-
firms not only that such emotions occur in the life of faith but that
such experiences are repeated, predictable, and expected. We have
been this way before.

What literary devices does this genre use to achieve its rhetorical effect?

Because psalms are poetry, we encounter in them an extraordinary
use of language. Laurence Perrine defines poetry as "a kind of language
that says *more* and says it *more intensely* than does ordinary language."[7]
Likewise, Robert Alter points to the semantic compactness of poetic
language:

Let me state the question about the form of the psalms in the most basic fashion: apart from the obvious utility of versification for texts that in many instances were actually sung, what difference does it make to the content of the psalms that they are poems? At this point I must confess allegiance, repeatedly confirmed by my own experience as a reader, to a notion about the language of poetry that was central to the American New Critics a generation ago and that more recently has been corroborated from a very different perspective by the Soviet literary semioticians: that poetry, working through a system of complex linkages of sound, image, word, rhythm, syntax, theme, idea, is an instrument for conveying densely-patterned meanings, and sometimes contradictory meanings, that are not readily conveyable through other kinds of discourse.[8]

Alter then approvingly cites the observation of Jurij Lotman that "if we understood better how a poem achieved the astonishing degree of 'information storage' that it does, our understanding of cybernetics might well be advanced." Alter further states,

The poetic medium [of the psalms] made it impossible to articulate the emotional freight, the moral consequences, the altered perception of the world that flowed from . . . monotheistic belief, in compact verbal structures that could in some instances seem simplicity itself. Psalms . . . were a common poetic genre [which] . . . became an instrument for expressing in a collective voice . . . a distinctive, sometimes radically new, sense of time, space, history, creation, and the character of individual destiny.[9]

We need to learn as preachers that when we are working with a psalm we are dealing with language and form which may appear to be simple and compact, but which, in fact, aims at creating a shift in the basic moral perception of the reader. Psalms operate at the level of the imagination, often swiveling the universe on the hinges of a single image. Sermons based on psalms should also seek to work their way into the deep recesses of the hearer's imagination.

The ways in which the psalms, through their poetic language, interact with the reader's perception, while complex and densely layered, are neither magical nor beyond analysis. When the preacher as interpreter performs a close reading of a psalm, certain poetic devices, characteristic ways of structuring language to achieve certain effects, begin to surface. Paying careful attention to these linguistic strategies can reveal to the exegete not only *how* the psalm is doing its work, but also much about what the psalm is seeking to say and to do.

Patrick D. Miller, Jr., in his immensely helpful volume *Interpreting the Psalms*, points to *balance*, the way in which two components in a poem are matched to each other, as one of the key aspects of psalmic poetry. "In biblical poetry this balance is traditionally understood to be manifest in three ways: rhythm, length, and meaning."[10] In each of these three ways balance is maintained by certain poetic devices. In the case of rhythm and length, the poet achieves balance by matching phrases in the poem according to both the number of syllables in each phrase and their meter (i.e., the frequency and arrangement of accented syllables). Miller notes that for the interpreter of the psalms these two devices are "not only problematic but less useful as far as understanding and illumination of the text are concerned."[11] For our purposes, it is sufficient to say that balanced rhythm and length are simply features of the psalm which make it "singable."

It is the third type of balance, the balance of meaning—the way in which subject matter is paired—that Miller underscores as aiding "the interpreter in gaining a sensitive, nuanced, and full reading of the passage under consideration."[12] The chief poetic device employed to achieve this type of balance is the well-known strategy of *parallelism*. If we are to approach the psalms with a literary eye, this poetic device clearly deserves our attention. Simply put, parallelism is a device in which a poet gives us part of a line, usually half, here called A, and then gives us the next part of the line, B, in such a way that the content of B has some connection to the content of A. Here is an obvious example from Ps. 73:1.

A Truly God is good to the upright,
B to those who are pure in heart.

A and B are parallel, that is, they are clearly connected to each other. But how? T. H. Robinson has suggested that the connection is one of synonymity or restatement: B is the same thing as A, only artfully rephrased. "So the poet goes back to the beginning again, and says the same thing once more, though he may partly or completely change the actual words to avoid monotony."[13]

It has long been recognized, though, that Robinson's view cannot account for the variety of parallel forms found in the psalms. Sometimes, it is true, the psalmist appears to restate in B what was said in

A; but on other occasions the poet appears to make a converse statement in B, or to elaborate upon what was said in A. The list of ways
in which A and B can be connected is almost endless.

An important advance in the understanding of the dynamics of
biblical parallelism has come through the work of James Kugel.[14]
Kugel saw that where parallelism was employed there was some
movement, an advance, between A and B. In his words, "A is so, and
what's more, B is so. . . . B typically *supports* A, carries it further,
backs it up, completes it, goes beyond it."[15]

A modern example of this is the statement, "My son is thirteen; he's
a teenager." While some people might think that the second sentence
is merely a broad restatement of the first, any parent of a teenager
would tell you that this interpretation badly misses the mark. The first
sentence tells us the boy's age; the second evokes the ethos of adolescence. The first sentence tells us how much time has passed since the
boy's birth; the second connotes the world of language, music, and
values in which the boy lives.

This pattern also occurs in biblical parallelism. When Ps. 12:2 says,
"Everyone utters lies to his neighbor," we are told that the basic fabric
of human community has become infected with deceit. When the
psalm continues with the parallel phrase, "with flattering lips and a
double heart they speak," we get a more specific description of just
what sort of lying is going on—unctuous puffery and duplicity. With
the first phrase we get the idea; with the second we can almost hear
the hollow words.

And when Ps. 22:2 states, "O my God, I cry by day, but thou dost
not answer; and by night, but find no rest," the second part of the
verse not only extends the first by making it clear that the crying to
God is ceaseless, it also exposes the theological texture of the longed-
for divine answer by showing that it embraces the hope for relief and
rest. B elaborates, extends, and advances A.

The value of this discussion for preaching on the psalms lies not in
the notion that sermons on psalms should themselves contain paral-
lelisms. They may, of course, but that is not the issue. My point is that
the preacher must pay attention in interpreting the psalm to the ways
in which the psalmist, through parallelism, unfolds and nuances the
central ideas and images around which the psalm is built. The effect
of parallelism on the reader is that those ideas and images begin to

take on life in her or his imagination. The sermon should seek to create a similar effect for hearers, even if the rhetorical strategies employed are quite different.

How in particular does the text under consideration, in its own literary setting, embody the characteristics and dynamics described in questions 1–3?

How may the sermon, in a new setting, say and do what the text says and does in its setting?

The final two questions may be jointly answered by carefully examining the text of Psalm 1. On the surface, this is a brief, uncomplicated psalm which sharply contrasts two ways of life—the righteous and the wicked. The psalm revolves around a pair of simple, clear, and straightforward images: the righteous person is like a tree, the wicked are like chaff.

Beneath this simplicity, however, lies a subtle and intricate use of poetic language. Robert Alter, in an exquisite exegesis of this psalm, attunes us to the way in which the verbs function in the text.[16] In v. 1 the righteous person is pictured as one who does *not* engage in certain actions. This kind of person does *not* walk, stand, or sit. By implication, of course, the wicked person *does* do all those things. There is a certain calisthenic quality to evil, and the wicked person is very animated indeed. "If he actually performed these actions, he would be on the constant move, headed toward the destination . . . of being ensconced in an assembly of fools."[17]

By contrast, the first phrase of v. 2 provides the righteous person with no verb at all, and the second phrase supplies a verb having to do with contemplation: "Rather in the Lord's teaching his delight; His teaching he murmurs day and night" (Alter's translation).

By the end of v. 2, then, the text has created a kinetic portrait of the wicked which is opposed to the relatively still picture of the righteous. Now come the central images, and they reinforce the verbs. The righteous person is like a tree—planted, fixed, anchored in place. The wicked, on the other hand, are the epitome of directionless movement, blown away like chaff. The righteous person "stands still," states Alter. "Indeed, . . . righteousness may depend upon [the] ability to stand still and reflect upon true things."[18]

Another aspect of these contrasting images, noted by Patrick Miller, among others, is that the psalmist uses far more space to describe the tree than the chaff. For three lines we stand before this tree and look. We see the flowing stream where it is planted (or, as Miller states, "transplanted"), observe its seasonal fruit, take in its thriving foliage. We spend a good deal of poetic time contemplating this tree. But as for the chaff—now we see it, now we don't. It gets one short clause. "Of the chaff there is nothing to say," notes Miller, "except that the wind drives it away to nothingness. That is all there is to chaff."[19]

The rest of the psalm now unfolds the truth we already know: the aimless, windblown wicked will never be able to stand in any place of permanence. They are swept into nothingness; their frenetic activity is a dance down the path to oblivion. "The wicked," observes Alter, "are not even accorded the dignity of being a proper grammatical subject of an active verb: windblown like chaff, whatever way they go on is trackless, directionless, doomed."[20] The Lord "knows" the way of the righteous, however, and here the psalmist employs a verb of deep intimacy. In terms of the fate of both the righteous and the wicked there "is a certain ambiguity, . . . in that the text does not say specifically what God does. . . . One senses that it is almost in the nature of things that the wicked way goes under."[21]

The rhetorical effect of the poetry of the psalm, then, is to create two contrasting spheres of activity in the awareness of the reader or hearer. One sphere is filled with frenetic, desperate, directionless motion which quickly fizzles out. The other is still, steady, calm, rich with the quiet and strong action of the wise person reflecting upon Torah. An effective sermon on this psalm may well be one which not only *describes* this contrast but also *recreates* its visual and emotional impact in the hearers.

The preacher, then, must search for examples of these two types of activity in contemporary experience. Where do we see fevered, windblown activity that ends in nothing? Perhaps in the latest magazine advertisement with a brooding picture of a thirty-year-old who epitomizes success and reminds the rest of us that time is passing us by. We are, the ad implies, not yet savvy enough, well-groomed enough, rich enough, famous enough, youthful enough, attractive enough, aggressive enough. The moment is urgent. The time has come for us to get our act together—to grasp, to search, to change, to adjust to the shifting winds of the prevailing *zeitgeist* before it is too late. "Like the chaff which the wind drives away . . ."

In Judith Guest's novel *Ordinary People* there is a character named Calvin Jarrett, a middle-aged attorney who is going through a major league version of what has come to be called a mid-life crisis. Not sure of himself, Calvin listens carefully whenever he overhears, at parties, in bars, or in casual conversation, someone say, "I'm the kind of man who . . ." He hopes to hear some wisdom he can apply to himself, but he is always disappointed. Finally he admits to himself, "I'm the kind of man who—hasn't the least idea what kind of man I am."[22] "Like the chaff which the wind drives away . . ."

4
PREACHING
on proverbs

"A soft answer turns away wrath, but a harsh word stirs up anger" is a famous biblical saying, a noble thought, and in some cases a useful piece of advice. But can it serve as the basis for a sermon? It is from the Book of Proverbs, of course, which for most preachers is nothing more than a deserted stretch of highway between Psalms and Ecclesiastes.

There are several reasons why the Book of Proverbs appears to be a dry and barren spot among lush biblical gardens. First, biblical proverbs appear to be largely devoid of theological content. There are exceptions, of course—"The fear of the Lord is the beginning of wisdom" (9:10) is one—but they are exceptions that prove the rule.[1] Most of the proverbs are pithy sayings that encapsulate the sort of common sense that people cross-stitch, frame, and hang on their kitchen walls.[2] "A word fitly spoken is like apples of gold in a setting of silver" (25:11) could just as well have appeared in *Poor Richard's Almanac* as in the Bible. Even when a proverb mentions God, it often appears to do so in a sentimental and mechanical way. "Wait for the Lord, and he will help you," the prescription of Prov. 20:22, could be the verse in a Hallmark greeting card.

Proverbs also seem excessively moralistic and, beyond that, overly concerned with preserving the status quo. "Love not sleep lest you come to poverty" (20:13) sounds like the sort of finger-shaking admonition given by a straw boss or the parent of a college freshman, or found in a fortune cookie. If the counsel, "My son, fear the Lord and the king, and do not disobey either of them" (24:21), is directed at those Christians who as a matter of conscience and faithful commitment are withholding the military-designated portion of their income tax, a debate will follow, and justifiably so.

Moreover, some of the biblical proverbs appear to be contradictory or even downright untrue. Proverbs 26:4 advises, "Answer not a fool according to his folly, lest you be like him yourself." Fair enough, except the very next proverb counsels, "Answer a fool according to his folly, lest he be wise in his own eyes." Which shall it be? And what about such insights as "The fear of the Lord prolongs life, but the years of the wicked will be short" (10:27) or "The reward for humility and fear of the Lord is riches and honor and life" (22:4)? We can all draw upon personal experience that gives the lie to those statements.

Small wonder then that even on those rare occasions when the lectionary includes a reading from the Book of Proverbs, most preachers scramble for higher homiletical ground, saying, in effect, "Leave the proverbs to Confucius; we'll stick with the prophets and the parables." This response, however, fails to recognize that there is more to a proverb than meets the eye. Proverbs are actually intricate literary expressions which are far more theological, less overtly moralistic, and more vitally related to lived experience than is apparent at first glance. To be sure, proverbs are difficult preaching texts, but to dismiss them as unfruitful is to overlook their true character and to silence a valuable voice within the chorus of faith.

Not only are proverbs a form of biblical discourse which should be recognized and honored, there is considerable evidence that people today often base their decisions, arrange their affairs, and form their values on proverb-like advice. Scan the shelves of any popular bookstore and you will find countless volumes of self-help books proffering advice on everything from sex to self-esteem, adolescence to assertiveness. These books say things such as, "No one can make you feel anything; you are the owner of your feelings"; "Giant strides toward fulfillment come one small step at a time"; "When someone tries to make you feel miserable, you should say, 'I think your misery wants company'"; or "Other people cannot be counted on to guard your interests; you have to look out for yourself." Such sayings are, in their own way, proverbs. Many of them are tragically unwise, but that does not alter the reality that people actually follow their advice.

People need the kind of portable and memorable wisdom of the nuts-and-bolts variety that a proverb is designed to provide. The question is not will people live by proverbs, but what kind of proverbs will they cherish. From time to time, Christian preaching should speak in the proverbial voice. The intricacies and power of the proverb genre, as well as its potential for preaching, will become plainer when examined in the light of the five interpretive questions.

What is the genre of the text?

The genre called proverb is composed of maxims, sayings, bywords expressed in brief, non-narrative form. In order to see more clearly what a proverb is, it is important to distinguish between a proverb and its literary cousin, the aphorism. While they look very much alike, an aphorism is more firmly connected to a particular situation and, perhaps, to the person who uttered it than is a proverb. "An aphorism," notes David Jasper, "implies a more literary origin in a specific author or source."[3] The saying "Foxes have holes, and birds of the air have nests, but the Son of Man has nowhere to lay his head" (Matt. 8:20) is an aphorism according to Jasper because it is clearly bound to the person and work of Jesus. However, Jesus' word, spoken earlier in Matthew, "Let the day's own trouble be sufficient for the day" (Matt. 6:34), moves closer to the category of proverb because of its more general range of application.[4]

This distinction between proverb and aphorism points to the tendency of the proverb to free itself from the constraints of a particular situation and so become a more general and public truth. James G. Williams says, "The proverb expresses the voice of the human subject as ancient, collective, wisdom."[5] Proverbs present themselves as truths to be applied to broad categories of human experience, rather than as observations drawn from and attached to solitary events.

It would be a mistake, though, to assume that because it floats free from the singular situation a proverb constitutes a claim to universal truth. A proverb is larger than one case, but not large enough to embrace all cases. The presence of contradictory proverbs within the same collection (e.g., Prov. 26:4–5, noted above) indicates that proverbs have an "upper limit" to their applicability. As wisdom, they transcend a single situation, but they do not have indiscriminate force to be applied anywhere and at all times. They speak to these cases, but not to those. They constitute "various 'occasions' of order rather than a total system."[6]

What is the rhetorical function of this genre?

The apparent rhetorical function of the proverb is to provide a general ethical guideline which the reader can then apply to various real-life circumstances. The proverb tells us in broad and memorable terms how to behave. Then we are charged with the responsibility of using it to plan the day.

This description of the function of the proverbs is a near miss, but a miss nonetheless. Proverbs *do* provide ethical guidance, but that is a second-order function. Their primary function lies in succinctly and graphically describing the way things are. Proverbs, like much of wisdom literature, are the product of times of relative stability. A proverb is created when a person of gifted discernment, the Sage, surveys various scenes in human experience and perceives a unifying theme which holds together these disparate moments. While most people viewing the same events would see only unrelated fragments of human activity, the Sage discovers an underlying motif. The proverb is in effect the Sage's attempt to announce that although human experience may look disconnected and episodic, there are actually linkages and continuities discernible beneath the surface. Most proverbs, in other words, are created primarily to answer not the question, What should we do? but rather the question, What is really going on here?

Take, for instance, the secular proverb, "A fool and his money are soon parted." It is easy to imagine how this saying originated. A variety of incompetent and irresponsible types were observed going about their business in a mixture of circumstances. Some were seen investing in get-rich-quick schemes. Others were spotted purchasing development property in a swamp or placing their life savings on a long shot at the track. Still others were observed buying rounds for everybody in the local tavern or getting in on the ground floor of the alchemy industry or making loans to relatives. The strategies were many, the financially disastrous results uniform; and a proverb was formed. What's going on here? "A fool and his money are soon parted."

What this means in terms of the rhetorical effect of proverbs is that proverbs push the readers in two directions simultaneously. They make a reference *backward* and a reference *forward*. They refer backward by summoning the reader to imagine the sort of experiences that led to the formation of the proverb. As Paul Ricoeur puts it, "Without being a narrative, the proverb implies a story"[7]—actually a set of stories. The proverb calls forth a series of everyday vignettes which are varied on the surface but bundled together by a deep harmony discerned through the proverb itself.

A proverb pushes the reader forward by implying that there are experiences yet to occur in which the proverb will apply. It is phrased in a way that makes it simple to remember and thus easy to transport to new events. As we have noted, though, a proverb does not "work" in every event of life. It fits only those experiences that are similar in key ways to the ones that called it forth. As William McKane describes it,

> [Proverbs] have a special kind of concreteness in virtue of which their meaning is open to the future and can be divined again and again in relation to a situation which calls forth the "proverb" as apt comment.[8]

A proverb seeks to form an "apt fit" with new situations, and it is here that it gains its ethical force. By first looking back to describe the way things have been it is then able to look toward the future and reveal what may occur in similar circumstances. To use another secular proverb, if a person has learned that it is true in some situations that "haste makes waste," the next time an urgent and feverish demand is encountered, this person will wonder, "Is *this* one of those times when 'haste makes waste'?" If the new situation fits the pattern, the wise person takes note of the insight provided by the proverb and lives accordingly.

To say this, though, is to indicate that the proverb is a risky rhetorical form because it depends to a high degree upon the reader's gift of and energy for discernment. The reader must perceive which constellation of experience is evoked by the proverb and which is not. The proverb "A wise person is cautious and turns away evil, but a fool throws off restraint and is careless" (14:16) implies that a wise person, encountering evil, will become cautious and turn away. By contrast, the fool will blunder forward into the midst of it. Around situations of evil, then, caution is wise and impulsiveness is folly, or as the modern version would have it, "Fools rush in where the wise fear to tread."

Now that's a good insight, but only in *certain* situations. In other circumstances speaking this proverb would have an oppressive effect. One can imagine it being quoted, for instance, as a reproof to Jesus as he ate and drank with sinners, as he demonstrated a seemingly impulsive lack of caution in his associations with those who were religiously and socially out-of-bounds. This is the irony of the proverbial form: it speaks wisdom, but it also *requires* wisdom to be rightly heard and employed. The Book of Proverbs itself says, "Like a lame man's legs, which hang useless, is a proverb in the mouth of fools" (26:7).

William McKane has pointed to the riskiness and rhetorical complexity of the proverb form by comparing it to another literary form, the riddle. Both, he says, are "cryptic," in the sense that their full meaning initially eludes the reader. The riddle, however, is designed to remain somewhat enigmatic. "The function of the riddle is to mystify and baffle." On the other hand, "The proverb may initially present a barrier to understanding, but when it is intuited it throws a brilliant light on the situations which it fits."[9] The goal of a proverb, then, is to achieve clarity through an intuitive leap. In a sense, though, a proverb moves more seductively toward its goal than does a riddle; a riddle advertises its mysterious character while the proverb conceals its beneath a veneer of the ordinary. So much is this the case, claims McKane, that "it is possible to assign a literal, pedestrian meaning" to a proverb. If the reader confuses the proverb's surface with its depth, the proverb is "generalized and the generalization does some justice to it, but it forecloses the meaning and destroys the hermeneutical openness which derives from its original concreteness."[10]

In order to understand the function of the proverb to provoke this sort of intuition, one additional factor must be mentioned, namely, what the proverb does not actually say, but rather implies. While prophecy and apocalypse are the literary genres of crisis, proverbs are the product of a culture in equilibrium. As such, they connote the cultural and theological consensus from which they come. This means that proverbs make sense only when seen as the foreground for which the whole fabric of the covenant relationship between God and the community serves as backdrop. Proverbs are spoken into a culture in which the religious character of life permeates every relationship, every corner of society. Household affairs, weights and measures, legal matters, personal reputations, politics—the "stuff" of proverbs—are all, by definition, religious and theological issues in proverbial literature. To listen to a proverb without at the same time hearing its covenantal background is to pry a gem from its setting. It is one thing to say that "poverty and disgrace come to him who ignores instruction" (13:18) in the *Wall Street Journal*, but quite another to say it in the context of the community of faith. In the latter case, every key word of the proverb becomes properly nuanced by the theological vocabulary of the faithful community.

What is, then, the rhetorical effect of a proverb? First, it evokes the whole matrix of faithful life. Like parental advice, it emerges from and depends upon an implied network of prior relationships. Next it sends readers on a search through their memories for apt examples. If the proverb is true, then where have we seen it exemplified? Finally, it provokes the imagination to wonder about other situations in which the wisdom of the proverb may apply and thereby provides an ethical guide for wise response. A proverb does all this in but a few words. A sermon based upon a proverb has more words with which to work, but it should do the same work and create the same effect as the proverb out of which it grows.

What literary devices does this genre employ to achieve its rhetorical effect?

The imagery in a proverb is usually rather homely and mundane, especially when compared with the "high poetry" of some of the psalms. Proverbs closely track the grooves of everyday, routine existence, and thus are filled with "sluggards," "quarreling spouses," "kind neighbors," "smooth talkers," people with "crooked minds" or "wise tongues," and kings who growl—as one would predict—"like lions." This sort of imagery does not push language to its limits so much as it pushes us to recall our familiar world of wise and foolish folk.

The imagery of the proverbs is less metaphoric, which would cause new connections and associations to erupt inexhaustibly, than it is synecdochic, in which a part stands for an identifiable whole. When a proverb says, "A truthful witness saves lives," we know that the phrase "a truthful witness" means to point beyond the individual to a class of truth-telling people. The part calls forth the whole, and moreover, these "truthful witnesses" are familiar to us from our experience. We know some of them, and we can call their names.

In addition to their typically earthbound imagery, the proverbs have a characteristic sentence structure: a single sentence composed of two parts. Robert Alter has noted that most of these one-sentence proverbs are constructed according to one of three general schemes:[11]

1. *Antithesis.* A two-part sentence in which the second part expresses the reverse of the first. Proverbs 14:33 is an example of this scheme: "Wisdom abides in the mind of a person of understanding, but it is not known in the heart of fools." The rhetorical effect of this structure is to create in the reader's mind opposing yet mutually informing dramas. On stage right appear people of understanding, while simultaneously on stage left, a cast of fools appears in another scene. The mind's eye roves back and forth between the two settings, comparing and contrasting.

2. *Elaboration.* A two-part sentence in which the second part intensifies the thought of the first or extends it in time. Proverbs 14:26 serves as an example: "In the fear of the Lord one has strong confidence, and his children will have a refuge." The rhetorical effect of this construction is to create a two-act play. In act 1 we see the actions of those who have strong confidence in the Lord. Act 2, set a generation later, unfolds the stories of their children, thus elaborating upon the wisdom we discovered in the initial act.

3. *Answer.* A two-part sentence in which the parts work together to create what seems to be the answer to a question which itself is not recorded. Some of these have a riddle-like quality, such as Prov. 11:22:

> Question (implied): What is like a gold ring in a pig's nose?
> Answer: Like a gold ring in a pig's nose is a beautiful woman with no discretion.

A more straightforward example is Prov. 21:3:

> Question (implied): What is more acceptable to the Lord than sacrifice?
> Answer: To do righteousness and justice, that is more acceptable to the Lord than sacrifice.

The rhetorical effect of this form is to bring to the reader's mind both the unspoken question and the human experiences that are the lived answer to that question.

Yet another rhetorical device employed in the proverbs is humor. Some of the proverbs are downright funny; they achieve their impact through exaggeration, thereby allowing the reader to laugh at life's folly. A strength of the *Today's English Version* translation of the Bible is that it captures much of the exaggerated, wisecracking character of some of the proverbs:[12]

Why doesn't the lazy man ever get out of the house? What is he afraid of? Lions? (Prov. 26:13)

Getting involved in an argument that is none of your business is like going down the street and grabbing a dog by the ears. (Prov. 26:17)

Human desires are like the world of the dead—there is always room for more. (Prov. 27:20)

How in particular does the text under consideration, in its own literary setting, embody the characteristics and dynamics described in the previous questions?

How may the sermon, in a new setting, say and do what the text says and does in its setting?

Before turning to the preaching possibilities present in proverbs, it is important to note that not all of the biblical proverbs are appropriate preaching texts. Because proverbs are embedded in a specific cultural setting, when that setting changes, its proverbs can become latent, awaiting a time when they may again become wisdom. Proverbs, as we have seen, cause the hearer to recall narratives, and a substantial shift in culture is, in effect, a change in a society's narrative repertoire. A proverb becomes latent when it can no longer make dynamic contact with the concrete circumstances that gave it birth. To speak such a proverb calls forth no stories or, worse, the wrong stories. The Book of Ecclesiastes is, in essence, an anti-proverbial document and thus stands as a canonical testimony to the truth that proverbs can lose their power to speak wisdom.

I would be gravely reluctant, for example, to preach a sermon on Prov. 23:13, "Do not withhold discipline from a child; if you beat him with a rod he will not die." There is constructive intent in the saying, of course, and the concept of "tough love" has merit. However, the reality of child abuse in our society screams so loudly that it is difficult to hear the wisdom of this proverb at this juncture in history. For the time being, its harshness of language calls forth the wrong ensemble of cultural stories and renders the proverb unwise.

Some proverbs, however, are still alive with wisdom, and by examining them closely, we may learn how a sermon based upon a proverb could be developed. One such example is Prov. 15:17: "Better is a dinner of herbs where love is than a fatted ox and hatred with it." The sentence structure is antithetical, summoning contrasting scenes in the reader's mind. Here is a table set with the simplest of foods but surrounded by people feasting upon the grace of a meal shared in love. There is a banquet table complete with silver, crystal, and the finest of meats. Servants are in watchful attendance; no wineglass goes unreplenished. But gloomy hatred fills the room; there is no warm laughter. The table conversation is cold. No one reaches out to touch another with affection. Amid the feast there is famine.

Building a sermon on this text involves, first of all, roaming through our memories for moments which parallel the two scenes. What do we see? What do we remember?

I remember a Sunday table set in a small farmhouse. I was a seminary student and had just preached a sermon in a country church for a congregation too small ever to afford a minister of "their own." Each week a different student would appear in their pulpit, and on this day I had been the one. After the service, a man had shyly asked if I would care to join his family for Sunday dinner, and now I was seated at his table.

His wife brought out several dishes of food, plain but joyfully served—corn, green beans, sliced tomatoes, a few pieces of beef. All from the farm, I was told. The man told me how glad they were that I was with them. He prayed a blessing, and we began to eat. In the middle of the meal, another man, wearing hunting clothes and holding a shotgun, appeared at the door. He had a brief conversation with my host, and then left. The farmer returned to the table and said, "He asked if he could hunt on my land, and I told him he could. I don't see this farm as *my* land, really. It's the Lord's land, and I'm supposed to take care of it. If someone else can get some pleasure from this place, I believe I should let them."

Somehow the gospel had taken root in that man's life, setting him free from the selfishness which consumes most of us. He was free to see himself not as an owner, but as a steward of what God had placed in his care. He could share his land and his food with the stranger. Who this farmer was and what he had said, I thought as I went back to my meal, formed the best sermon preached that day. "Better is a dinner of herbs where love is . . ."

I also think of Garrison Keillor's description of his "storm home" in the imaginative memoir *Lake Wobegon Days*. He tells us there that the principal of the school, Mr. Detman, fearful of a winter blizzard during the school day, had assigned each student from the country a storm home in town near the school. If a blizzard struck, each child was to go to his storm home. Keillor writes:

> Mine was the Kloeckls', an old couple who lived in a little green cottage by the lake. She kept a rock garden on the lake side, with terraces of alyssum, pansies, petunias, moss roses, rising to a statue of the Blessed Virgin seated, and around her feet a bed of marigolds. It was a magical garden, perfectly arranged; the ivy on the trellis seemed to move up in formation, platoons of asters and irises along the drive, and three cast-iron deer grazed in front: it looked like the home of the kindly old couple that the children lost in the forest suddenly come upon in a clearing and know they are lucky to be in a story with a happy ending. That was how I felt about the Kloeckls, after I got their name on a slip of paper and walked by their house and inspected it, though my family might have wondered about my assignment to a Catholic home, had they known. We were suspicious of Catholics, enough to wonder if perhaps the Pope had ordered them to take in little Protestant children during blizzards and make them say the Rosary for their suppers. But I imagined the Kloeckls had personally chosen me as their storm child because they liked me. "Him!" they had told Mr. Detman. "In the event of a blizzard, we want that boy! The skinny one with the thick glasses!"
>
> No blizzard came during school hours that year, all the snowstorms were convenient evening or weekend ones, and I never got to stay with the Kloeckls, but they were often in my thoughts and they grew large in my imagination. My Storm Home. Blizzards aren't the only storms and not the worst by any means. I could imagine worse things. If the worst should come, I could go to the Kloeckls and knock on their door. "Hello," I'd say. "I'm your storm child."

"Oh, I know," she'd say. "I was wondering when you'd come. Oh, it's good to see you. How would you like a hot chocolate and an oatmeal cookie?"

We'd sit at the table. "Looks like this storm is going to last awhile."

"Yes."

"Terrible storm. They say it's going to get worse before it stops. I just pray for anyone who's out in this."

"Yes."

"But we're so glad to have you. I can't tell you. Carl! Come down and see who's here."

"Is it the storm child??"

"Yes! Himself, in the flesh!"[13]

Better is a dinner of herbs—or hot chocolate and oatmeal cookies—where love is . . .

I also remember the experience of a friend, a minister. He was approached by a member of his church, an elderly man, the sort of loyal layperson given to deep devotion and constant fidelity to the life of the church but not to sophisticated theological talk. "Preacher," he began, "I want you to correct my thinking."

"How's that?" responded my friend.

"Last week, during communion, I had a strange feeling, a funny notion, and I want you to set me straight about it."

"What happened?"

"It was when the little pieces of bread were being passed around. You had said something about this being a feast for God's family, and when I took the bread I began to think that we weren't the only ones here. I felt that my mother and father were here, too. In my mind I saw my brother, Sam, and my grandparents, and all those who've gone before me. Preacher, I know all those people are dead and gone, and I'll see them in heaven someday, but I couldn't get them out of my mind. I felt they were right there at that table last Sunday with us. It was a good feeling, preacher, but I know I need you to straighten me out."

"No, I don't need to straighten you out," said my friend slowly. "What you felt was true." Better is a dinner of grape juice and bread where love is . . .

I also think, though, of other meals. I remember the strained rehearsal dinner for a wedding bitterly opposed by the bride's parents. I remember with pain the family meal at which I was so blind to what was happening that I pressed what I thought was harmless teasing to the point of forcing one of my children away from the table in humiliation and tears. I remember being told by a woman of the time when, in the middle of a lavish meal in a fancy restaurant, her husband had informed her that there was someone else and that he would not be going home with her that night. I remember the meal where Judas slipped away from the table and disappeared into the darkness. "Better is a dinner of herbs where love is than a fatted ox and hatred with it."

A sermon on this proverb could move in just this way. Narratives, vignettes, story-like threads that the proverb tugs from the fabric of everyday life would be told, each thread punctuated by the proverb itself, quoted as an interpretive refrain.

Now the proverb completes its task. Because of what it allows us to remember, we think of the next table where we will take our places. The sermon can make the same temporal shift, enabling the hearer to anticipate new places in experience where the wisdom of the proverb can provide guidance. The proverb, which has sent us back in memory, now sends us forward into the future, forward to wonder what the true meat of our next meal will be. Our imagination is fixed not upon the linen tablecloth or the fine china but upon the people who are gathered there, the faith we share, the love possible within this moment of fellowship. Are we wise enough to know how to receive this moment, to savor its grace? Or will we walk away from this, God's everyday banquet of mercy, with full stomachs and empty hearts? "Better is a dinner of herbs where love is than a fatted ox and hatred with it."

5
PREACHING
on narratives

There are two odd things about the Bible and stories. The first odd thing about biblical stories is that there are so many of them. There are battle stories, betrayal stories, stories about seduction and treachery in the royal court, stories about farmers and fools, healing stories, violent stories, funny stories and sad ones, stories of death, and stories of resurrection. In fact, stories are so common in Scripture that some students have claimed, understandably but incorrectly, that the Bible is exclusively a narrative collection. This is an exaggeration, of course—there is much non-narrative material in the Bible—but the claim that the Bible is a "story book" is not far off the mark. There is, indeed, a narrative understructure to the Bible, and even its non-narrative portions bear a crucial relationship to the "master" stories of Scripture.

The reason this is odd is that religions do not necessarily depend upon narrative to convey their thought. Lists of precepts, thematic essays, systematic theologies, riddles, or even probing and open-ended questions are among the literary options available to teachers of religion. Stories are, in some ways, notoriously ambiguous and inefficient devices for conveying truth, and it is a puzzle worth pondering that narrative is the dominant form of choice for biblical writers.

The second odd thing about the Bible and stories has been expressed by Adele Berlin: "It is ironic that, although telling is so important in the biblical tradition, there is no word for story. There are words for songs and oracles, hymns and parables . . . [but] there is nothing to designate narrative *per se*."[1] It is odd that the Bible does not pause to reflect upon or even to coin a term for its most prevalent literary form.

These observations seem less odd when we look more closely at the literary and theological circumstances which gave rise to the biblical writings. As recent scholarship has increasingly documented, the biblical writers were literary artists of considerable skill and sophistication who were not unacquainted with the creative, even playful, possibilities of language. Biblical writings of all sorts, therefore, display strong literary and poetic qualities. These artistic tendencies were not given free rein, however, but were disciplined by the larger theological purposes which governed the writers' work. Stories are so abundant in Scripture precisely because the biblical writers were both artists *and* theologians. The narrative literary form is a logical outgrowth of the interaction between the artistic freedom of the biblical writers and their theological world view.

The novelist Reynolds Price once remarked that most of the world's chatter—novels, jokes, plays, songs—represents a craving for the one truly sufficient story. "We are satisfied," he says, "only by the one short tale we feel to be true: *History is the will of a just God who knows us.* "[2] Robert Alter has described the basic theological quest of the biblical writers in similar terms, as a desire "to reveal the enactment of God's purpose in history."[3] This high theological purpose placed biblical writers, in Alter's view, in the middle of an interplay between two forces. On the one hand, they believed in the unwavering character of God's will, the constancy of the divine promise, and were certain that God had a harmonious plan for creation. On the other hand, they knew that human history was actually disorderly, human freedom was random, and human beings were stubborn and resistant.[4] Narrative became a particularly apt literary form for capturing the fullest possible range of the interplay between these opposing forces. As Alter maintains,

> The biblical tale might usefully be regarded as a narrative experiment in the possibilities of moral, spiritual, and historical knowledge, undertaken through a process of studied contrasts between the variously limited knowledge of the human characters and the divine omniscience quietly but firmly represented by the narrator. . . .
> [The biblical writer's] typically monotheistic decision is to lead us to know as flesh-and-blood knows: character is revealed primarily through

speech, action, gesture, with all the ambiguities that entails; motive is frequently, though not invariably, left in a penumbra of doubt. . . .

At the same time, however, the omniscient narrator conveys a sense that personages and events produce a certain stable significance, one which in part can be measured by the varying distances of the characters from divine knowledge, but the course through which some of them are made to pass from dangerous ignorance to necessary knowledge of self and other, and of God's ways.[5]

In short, biblical writers produced narratives not in a vacuum, but out of the struggle to produce a fit between the literary form and their theological world view. Meir Sternberg, in *The Poetics of Biblical Narrative*, is quite specific about the forces in play upon biblical writers. They were regulated, he maintains, by "a set of three principles: ideological, historiographic, and aesthetic."[6] This is an intriguing set of principles because, like literary Angelfish, each tends to be aggressive, territorial, and intolerant of the others. Taken in the abstract, these principles are natural rivals, tending to encourage the production of quite distinctive types of literatures. Ideological writing tends to be dogmatic, didactic literature that eliminates aesthetic finesse and files smooth those rough edges of historical fact that do not fit doctrinal pattern. Pure historiography, says Sternberg, "would like nothing better than to tack fact onto fact in an endless procession, marching across all artistic and ideological design." The concern of aesthetic writing is not history or dogma, but only the creative and artistically playful use of language. Each of these three principles if given free rein "would pull in a different direction and either win the tug of war or tear the work apart."[7]

Biblical narrative, however, manages to bring these three impulses into cooperative interaction, in part by allowing history to mediate between the other two principles. Biblical writers were historically oriented, but—and this is a crucial exception—they did not have a notion of history as "one damned thing after another." They saw history as grounded in the control and providence of God; therefore, history could not be told as a random series of disconnected events. Since history had a shape, it had to be told in a way that was "plotted" like a story. This view opened the way for a full display of narrative aesthetics. When history is seen as theologically shaped, it takes an artist to tell the story.

Not just any sort of narrative would do, though, because this God who acts in history is separated from humanity by a chasm labeled "knowledge." God is omniscient; human beings are limited in wisdom—and the stories which embody this view of reality must be told in such a way as to disclose this truth. The result, in Sternberg's view, is a kind of narrative literature, a set of biblical stories which create in the reader a process of reading which emulates the faithful discovery that an omniscient God keeps covenant with human beings, whose lives nonetheless remain limited and fragmented.

> [Ideology, historiography, and aesthetics] join forces to originate a strategy of telling that casts reading as a drama, interpretation as an ordeal that enacts and distinguishes the human predicament. . . .
> History unrolls as a continuum of discontinuities, a sequence of non-sequiturs, which challenge us to repair the omissions by our native wit. Through a mimesis of real-life conditions of inference, we are surrounded by ambiguities, baffled and misled by appearances, reduced to piecing fragments together by trial and error, often left in the dark about essentials to the very end. . . . With the narrative become an obstacle course, its reading turns into a drama of understanding— conflict between inferences, seesawing, reversal, discovery and all. The only knowledge perfectly acquired is the knowledge of our limitations. It is by a sustained effort alone that the reader can attain at the end to something of the vision that God has possessed all along: to make sense of the discourse is to gain a sense of being human.[8]

Alter and Sternberg help us see not only why narrative is so prominent in the Bible but also why biblical stories are told as they are. Through its literary form and dynamics, biblical narrative embodies in a basic and apt way the general theological view of reality held by the biblical writers. What is more, the way in which a reader reads and comes to understand a biblical narrative is congruent with the ways in which a person comes to "read" and understand all of the ambiguities of history as governed by the will of God. This correspondence between the narrative form and the biblical writer's basic perception of reality may also tell us why there is no biblical term for "story." In the Bible, narrative is not a device; it is an expression of the way things are. The biblical writers do not pause to say, "And now I am going to tell you a story," as if narration were an interruption of some otherwise more fundamental task. The first-order work of the biblical writers was to "reveal the enactment of God's purposes in history." What resulted was not a reflection upon narrative, but narrative itself. In short, theology led to literary form. We can now examine the ways in which the literary form called biblical narrative impacts readers.

What is the genre of the text?

People tell stories—and recognize them—without thinking much about them. We know the difference between a person at the dinner table telling a story and that same person saying things that are not stories, such as making a request ("Please pass the bread") or giving an opinion ("John Updike's new novel is his best yet"). But what exactly is a story? How do we recognize one when we hear it?

Robert Scholes devised a playful multiple-choice test to determine the basic definition of story.[9] Which of the following, he asked, would qualify as stories?

1. The king was healthy but he became ill, and though he tried every medicine in the kingdom, he finally died.
2. The king was healthy but then he became ill and then he died.
3. The king was healthy but then he became ill.
4. The king was healthy but then he died.
5. The king was ill and then he died.
6. The king was ill and then the queen died.
7. The king was ill and then John Smith died.

Scholes says that (1), although certainly not a very interesting story, is surely a narrative. Number (7), the listing of two apparently unrelated events, the king's illness and Smith's death, is clearly non-narrative; it may be a chronicle, but it is not a story. But where, on the downward path from (1) to (7), do we cross the border and leave the land of story?

We can try to answer this question by first asking what it is about (1) that signals to us as readers that it is a miniature story? First, it involves the passing of time. A story is not like a still life painting. An exquisite description of a weatherbeaten farmhouse would not be a story because nothing happens. In a story the frame is not frozen; there is movement through time.

But it is not enough to say just that stories describe the passing of time. All of the sentences on the list involve temporal movement. What sets (1) apart is not only that events occur as time passes but also that the events are linked to each other in significant ways.

Stories do not merely say that this happened, then that happened, and then another thing happened. They say *because* this happened, that happened. In (1), a situation developed which cried out for action (the once healthy king became ill); because of this, the action was taken (he tried every medicine in the kingdom); this action had a result which seems to be complete or finished (the king died). A story is a chain of connected events which leads to a conclusion.

This matter of leading to a conclusion is an important characteristic of a story. Readers instinctively sense when a story is complete and when one is unfinished. If (1) had ended with the line "and the king finally got well" instead of "he finally died," it would still have been a story because the sequence of events would have led to a result which seemed finished. Suppose, though, that (1) had closed with the statement, "but the king got no better at all." Most readers would say, "So what did he do then?" In other words, this narrative would not be finished and therefore could not claim to be story.

But what if the example read as follows?

The king was healthy, but he became ill. Even though every medicine in the kingdom was offered to him, he refused them all, and because his illness went untreated he finally died.

Would this too be a story? Yes, because a situation develops which cries out for action, the necessary action is described, and that action (in this case the mysterious refusal to take medicine) leads to a finished result, a conclusion. In other words, a story is a pathway between points A and B. Point A is the opening section in which an unresolved situation is set out. B is the point at which the resolution of the situation seems to a reader to be complete. In between lie the actions which move the reader between the two points.

What is implied here can be put even more simply: A story is a series of events which can be seen as having a beginning, a middle, and an end. It is important, of course, that we recognize the logical relationships among those three parts. The beginning of a story always describes a situation of need that must be addressed through an action of some kind. The middle grows out of the beginning by describing what is done about this needed action. The end in turn grows out of the middle by showing what happens as a result of the action taken in the middle. At the same time, the end relates to the beginning by resolving its situation of need. The end allows the reader to say, "Yes, this is 'the end,'" either by showing how the need described in the beginning has been met (the king got well) or by describing how all reasonable opportunity for future action has been cut off (the king died).[10] This fundamental understanding of a story eliminates from our test list (2) through (7) because each lacks either a middle, an end, or the necessary linkages to hold the parts together.

Clearly, then, stories are not merely descriptions of the passing of time. They are ways of *organizing time*, of giving logical and meaningful shape to the otherwise incoherent occurrence of events. A storyteller, in effect, says to us, "Listen, life is not really a meaningless jumble of disjointed experiences. Events are not always like boulders crashing down from a mountaintop, without mercy and beyond control, never really ending, only running out of energy. Sometimes things happen that can go one way or another. And what people do makes a difference in when they end and how they end. Let me tell you about one. 'Once upon a time. . . .'"

This is important because it means that stories organize time in the same way we organize the passing moments of our lives. When I get up in the morning and head out the door, I do not understand myself to be heading out into a pinball-machine-world of random and meaningless events. To the contrary, I think of myself as "beginning the day," entering into a kind of open-ended story in which I am one of the principal characters. What I do or do not do will greatly affect how the day ends. What is more, as the narrator of my own story I must decide which of the millions of events happening around me are connected to the logic of the story and which are not. I have to take all of the "ands" of my raw experience and decide which of them are really "becauses." On most days the acorn falling at my feet as I walk to the office will be filtered out of the narrative, whereas the class I meet later in the day and the conversation with a colleague over coffee will become deeply woven into the plot. On other more leisurely days the falling acorn may be brought into the center of an episode.

Because we live our lives as implicit narratives, and because others do also, we are eager to exchange life-experience stories. These stories are almost always more than they appear to be on the surface. To relate a part of our story to another person is not only to tell what happened but also to reveal how we make sense of life, how and what we decide is important and not important, and how we respond to the ethical decisions arising from events.

Even when others do not tell us their stories, we try to guess what those stories may be. Suppose we are walking through an airport and we spot a young man in a Navy uniform dash out of a plane and into the arms of a waiting woman. Or, like Jimmy Stewart in Alfred Hitchcock's *Rear Window*, we see through the window of the apartment across the way a woman eating a tearful meal by herself at a table set for two. What do we do with such experiences? We create stories around them in our imaginations. The young man has been away at sea for many months, we tell ourselves, and now has been joyfully reunited with the woman he loves. The woman in the apartment has been stood up, we guess, and now must eat her meal in bitter disappointment. None of this may be true, of course—the couple in the airport may be brother and sister, the woman in the apartment may be weeping as she eats raw onions while waiting for her gin rummy partner—but we spin these tales anyway in an effort to make sense out of what we have seen. Without the stories to organize the events of life, they are just random and disconnected blips in time.

We are curious about other people's stories not only because they are often interesting but also because they have the power to suggest possibilities for our own lives. Consider the following rabbinic story:

> In far-off Krakow, back when sleep was still often disturbed by dreams, there lived one Eisik, son of Yekel, a poor man whose family seldom ate their fill. One night in a dream he saw the distant city of Prague, noticing that there was a certain bridge over the Vltava with a treasure buried beneath it. The dream was so vivid that he couldn't forget it, especially when it kept recurring every night for two weeks. So finally, in order to exorcise the demon from his mind, he determined to walk all the way to Prague to see for himself.
>
> After several days he arrived in the city—recognizing it from his dream—found the bridge and went underneath it to locate the treasure. But suddenly a soldier grabbed him by the back of the neck and took him away to prison for questioning. There he was asked what he was doing prowling under the bridge. Not knowing what else to say, he blurted out the truth. He said he was looking for a treasure that he had imagined in a dream.
>
> Impulsively the soldier broke into laughter and scoffed, "You stupid Jew! Don't you know that you can't trust what you see in your dreams?

Why, for the last two weeks I myself have dreamt that far away in Krakow, in the house of one Jew, Eisik, son of Yekel, there is a treasure buried under the stove in his kitchen. But wouldn't it be the most idiotic thing in the world if I were to go all the way there to look for it? In a city where there must be a hundred Eisiks, sons of Yekel! Where one could waste a lifetime looking for a treasure that doesn't exist!" Still laughing, the soldier gave him a kick and let him go. Then Eisik, son of Yekel, walked back to Krakow, to his own home, where he moved the stove in his kitchen, found the treasure buried there, and lived to a ripe old age as a rich man.[11]

This story is more than merely interesting; it contains wisdom and moral insight. When we finish reading it, we are probably not content to say, "Wasn't that fascinating. What happened to Eisik?" We will no doubt move beyond mere curiosity to say to ourselves, "If life is in any way like that story, what does this mean for me? What am I dreaming about? What am I missing around me?" In other words, we place each new story alongside our own narratives, allowing them to speak to each other.

Now the question we must ask is, What happens to us as a result of this interaction between stories?

What is the rhetorical function of this genre?

What does a story *do* to a reader? The answers are virtually infinite. At the risk of oversimplification, though, it can be said that a good story creates its impact in one of two ways: (1) by making the reader one of the characters or (2) by making a claim concerning the nature of life, a claim about which the reader must make a decision.

Identification with Character

In *Lost in the Cosmos*, Walker Percy asks, "Why is it that, when you are shown a group photograph in which you are present, you always (and probably covertly) seek yourself out?"[12] Providing a full answer to this question, as Percy suggested, will involve probing one of the great mysteries of the self, but the fact is we *do* indeed look for our own face in the picture. The same dynamic is at work when we read and hear stories. A friend tells of her recent bout with a strange virus that produced vague listlessness and sapped her energy, and we immediately begin to check ourselves for symptoms. We read a newspaper story about a person much like ourselves who was attacked in his home by an intruder, and we wonder if we should put a better lock on our door. "Could this be our story, too?" we ask.

The impact of biblical stories is often a result of this dynamic of identification with character. As Amos Wilder noted,

> Perhaps the special character of the stories in the New Testament lies in the fact that they are not told for themselves, that they are not only about other people, but that they are always about us. They locate us in the very midst of the great story and plot of all time and space, and therefore relate us to the great dramatist and storyteller, God himself. . . . This question of identification arises with every story we read, whether folk-story, epic, or modern novel. We identify with the hero or the villain, in their actions or in their fortunes.[13]

When we identify with a character in a story, whatever happens to that character happens to us at the level of imagination. One way to observe this process of identification with character, and at the same time to stimulate a vigorous discussion, is to read the story of Mary and Martha (Luke 10:38–42) to a group of church folk and ask them whether they see themselves as "Marys" or "Marthas." Those who identify with "Martha" may be angered by Jesus' response, even think it unfair, but nonetheless hear his confronting words spoken to *them*, "Martha, Martha, you are anxious and troubled by many things."

In most cases, identification with character occurs willingly and spontaneously. The reader intuits that a character in a story is in important respects like himself or herself. The character is perceived to be one who, in the words of literary critic Norman Holland, shares an "adaptation and lifestyle"[14] similar to the reader's, so the reader, in a literary sense, can "become" the character. Storytellers work at presenting a character in just the way that will enable the reader to say, "I'm like that."

A variation on this theme of identification with character involves those stories which present a certain character as a model or ideal. These stories say or imply at the end, "Now go and do likewise." While we may not initially identify with the character, the function of the story is to create the desire in us to be like the person. We hear the story of the passenger in the airplane that crashed into the Potomac River, who could have saved himself by swimming to the bank of the river, but he chose to remain in the icy waters helping others to be rescued, at the cost of his own life. While most of us do not identify *with* him, we desire to be *like* him. The Bible, too, gives us stories of faith and courage, and characters worthy of emulation. The parable of the Good Samaritan and some of the stories in the Book of Daniel are among the biblical narratives that work in this fashion.

Response to a Claim about Life

Sometimes stories create their impact not by asking us to see ourselves as one of the characters but by setting forth a "slice of life," by declaring, "This is how the world really is," and demanding a response from the reader to the question, Is it true or not? We each have stories by which we define our identity and shape our life. Each new story we encounter is placed alongside the old stories for comparison. Sometimes the new story confirms our world view, but on other occasions it challenges that world—and we must choose in which world we will live.

One such story is of a well-known scientist and inventor who chose to live a very simple, even austere life. His inventions brought him much wealth, but he gave most of his fortune away. Indeed, he made it a rule never to turn down a request from anyone who needed money, and as a result was often solicited by con artists as well as by the genuinely needy. He realized this, of course, but said that he would rather give money to a person who did not deserve it than risk refusing money to a person who was truly needy.

This story makes a claim upon us even though we may not identify with its main character. Its world is one in which the meeting of human need is so crucial, urgent, and joyfully done that more ordinary virtues, like prudence, are less important. The important question is not, Do I see myself as this man? but rather, Do I understand the world that way, and if not, should I?

Biblical stories often generate their impact by creating an alternative world in the imagination and challenging the reader to make a decision about it. Some time ago I saw a man recite, in dramatic fashion, the whole of the Gospel of Mark. At various times I found myself siding with one character or another, but my overall impression was that I was in the presence of a very vigorous, very misunderstood, very rough-edged, very Markan Jesus. The skillful recreation of Mark's storytelling genius allowed this powerful and in many ways threatening Jesus to stand forth, and I was confronted with precisely the issues that lie at the heart of Mark's Gospel: Is *that* the "Christ, the Son of God"? Do I understand him? Is it possible to understand him? Would I follow him to the death? What will happen if I do? If I don't?

There are other stories, however, which are far more didactic and which seem to be designed to bring the reader into an encounter not with a totally new world view but with one focused truth. Pronouncement stories, for example, as Robert Tannehill has observed, are rhetorically shaped to showcase a brief saying, such as, "A prophet is not without honor, except in his own country," or "No one who puts his hand to the plow and looks back is fit for the kingdom of God." This shaping is part of an overall narrative strategy in which the author hopes to invite the reader to shift from one attitude, sometimes expressed in the beginning of the story, to the new attitude embodied in the pronouncement.[15]

What literary devices does this genre employ to achieve its rhetorical effect?

A good story makes possible the subtle interplay of many narrative ingredients at several levels. There are basic literary dynamics to which a preacher should be attentive when exploring a narrative text.

Narrative Techniques

The narrator, the story*teller*, controls much of the reading process. A story may begin in a variety of ways; it is the narrator who decides which way. Many details could be included in a story; it is the narrator who selects what we will and will not be told, and in what order. The narrator can tease us, surprise us, teach us, confuse us, mislead us, put us "in the know," or keep us in suspense.

In general, biblical narrators are both in the background and omniscient. They are in the background in the sense that with few exceptions (e.g., the "we" passages in Acts) the biblical storytellers are not characters in the stories. In John D. MacDonald's mystery novels, the hero, Travis McGee, tells his own story ("I reached across the desk and handed him Boggs' card"), but biblical narrators are voices outside of the stories. They are omniscient because they know everything about the story, often more than some of the characters know.

John, for instance, knows that Pilate is afraid of the mob outside the praetorium. Luke knows that Jesus can read the minds of the Pharisees in the synagogue. The writer of 1 Samuel knows that Jonathan loved David "as his own soul."

If the narrator knows everything, the questions become, When is the reader informed? What do we learn through and with the characters? What are we told in advance? In the Gospel of Mark, for instance, we are told in the first line that Jesus is "Christ, the Son of God." We know this, in other words, before the characters do, and as we read we wait patiently for them to discover what we already know. "Who then is this, that even the wind and the sea obey him?" ask the disciples on the now calmed sea. We know because the narrator has told us and has thereby distanced us from the story's characters. We know more than they do and, in a literary sense, are even superior to them. Seven and one-half chapters later, when Peter finally blurts out, "You are the Christ" (8:29), we have the satisfaction of seeing a character arrive at last at the knowledge we have possessed all along.

But then the disciples are told that "whoever would save his life will lose it; and whoever loses his life for my sake and the gospel's will save it" (8:34). We did not know that. Suddenly the distance the narrator built between us and the disciples disappears, and we are on equal and fearful footing. Our confident foreknowledge is lost in the shock of reading Jesus' call to follow along the way of the cross.

Another characteristic of biblical narrative is its spare style. Biblical stories are told leanly and economically, with a minimum of detail. We read, "He opened the book of the prophet Isaiah, and found the place," not "Carefully, but firmly, he opened the book of the prophet Isaiah, finding there the ancient words so often read and so well loved." This narrative reticence invites readers to "flesh out" the story in their own imaginations and highlights those details which *are* provided. When a biblical narrator does supply a detail, it merits our full attention. In Genesis 48, for instance, when old Jacob, near death, his sight failing, reaches out to bless Joseph's two sons, the narrator tells us that Jacob crossed his hands. This is a detail worth noting since it meant that Jacob's right hand fell upon the younger son, not on the older one as would have been expected. Again, in the midst of the feeding of the five thousand in the wilderness, Mark pauses to note that the multitude sat down on the "green grass." Why does he describe the color of the grass as green but not the sky as blue or the sand as yellow? Is Isaiah's vision of the wilderness in blossom even now being realized?

Narrators control the readers' point of view not only by setting the mood of the story but also by pointing the narrative camera in a specific direction, thereby giving the readers a certain angle of vision. When the author of 2 Samuel writes, "It happened, late one afternoon, when David arose from his couch and was walking upon the roof of the king's house, that he saw from the roof a woman bathing, and the woman was very beautiful," the camera follows David, looks over his shoulder so that we see what he sees, whom he sees. We are guided toward and experience the event with David. When John says, "On the third day there was a marriage at Cana in Galilee, and the mother of Jesus was there," the camera surveys the wedding scene and then comes to rest upon Mary thereby hinting that this is to be, at least to some degree, a story about *her*.

Character Development

Like most narrative literature, the Bible contains both "round" and "flat" characters, that is, characters like Moses who are complex and richly developed, and characters who are nothing more than a single, consistent trait—Herod, for example. Even when a biblical story includes a round character, the same reticence noted earlier concerning narrative technique applies to character development. Adele Berlin has observed that the biblical writers avoid describing physical appearance or emotional state in favor of using terse labels—"rich," "old," "wise," "lame," "strong." Each descriptive term, Berlin notes, seems to be selected "not to enable the reader to visualize the character, but to enable him to situate the character in terms of his place in society, his own particular situation, and his outstanding traits—in other words, to tell what kind of person he is."[16]

We also get to know characters through dialogue, a technique for character development preferred by biblical writers. Robert Alter has suggested that one of Esau's lines to Jacob might well be translated, "Let me cram my maw with this red . . . red stuff."[17] The narrator does not need to tell us that Esau is a rube; Esau has told us himself.

Plot Designs

Narrative plots are intricate and complex, but the preacher can expose something of the plot dynamic by exploring the three basic components: the beginning, the middle, and the end. What is the need established in the beginning? How does the end address this need? What is the path—the middle—by which the narrative moves from beginning to end?

Consider, for example, the fascinating and intricate story in Mark 3:1-6 about the Sabbath healing of the man with the withered hand. This is not a simple healing story in which there is a need (illness), an action (healing), and a result (restoration). The narrator sets up the beginning in a more complex way:

> Again he entered the synagogue, and a man was there who had a withered hand. And they watched him to see if he would heal him on the Sabbath so that they might accuse him. (vv. 1-2)

What this says is that Jesus walked into the synagogue and encountered *two* needs: the illness of the man and the desire of "them" (i.e., the Pharisees) to obtain grounds for an accusation. One action is called for—healing—and it will satisfy both needs. The only question is whether or not Jesus will perform it. If we peek at the end of the story, we see that both needs have been met and the dilemma set out in the beginning has been "resolved":

> His hand was restored. The Pharisees went out, and immediately held counsel with the Herodians against him, how to destroy him. (vv. 5-6)

We can imagine an alternative ending to this story:

> His hand was restored, and because of Jesus' favor with all the people, the Pharisees could say nothing against him.

This ending too would provide a finish to the story set in motion by the beginning, but it would be a different story requiring a different middle, a different plot. The original story, however, will not lead us to Jesus' popularity. It will not tell us that the congregation was "astonished" or that people exclaimed, "Who is this who can even heal the diseased?" The original story will not take us on a path which leads to healing and acclaim; it will take us on a path which leads to healing and premeditated murder.

When we explore this path—the "middle" of the plot—we see that Jesus addresses both parties in "need." To the broken man, he says, "Come here," thus preparing the scene for action. To the Pharisees, he says, "Is it lawful on the Sabbath to do good or to do harm, to save life or to kill?" That is not the way they would have posed the question, of course. In their view, the options were not to do good or to do harm, but to practice medicine on the Sabbath or to do nothing. Jesus refuses this morally neutral use of language and its implied view of the law. The law either gives life or takes it away. Those are the only two choices; the law is not inert. Jesus' words also expose— as the narrator has already told us—the Pharisees' desire on that Sabbath, the choice to which their view of the law has already led them: to do harm and to kill.

The Pharisees are silent, a silence which betrays their moral choice. What could cause a person to construe the law in such a way? The narrator tells us, "Jesus looked around at them with anger, grieved at their hardness of heart."

"Stretch out your hand," Jesus said, and in a single healing action he gave the man what he needed and gave the Pharisees what they wanted.

Other Elements

In addition to narrative technique, character development, and plot development, there are other literary techniques evident in biblical stories. These include:

1. *Word Choice*. A biblical storyteller may use a word or phrase which carries a larger, symbolic meaning. When John says that it was *night* when Judas left the last supper, the term clearly carries a theological connotation: Night conveys all that opposes the light of God's glory in Jesus Christ.

2. *Location*. Places may be invested with symbolic meaning. Mark, for example, uses the word 'eremos (wilderness) six times in chapter 1 alone, creating a place of spiritual as well as geographical significance. And often, when the Markan Jesus wishes to communicate privileged information to his disciples (to the church?), he goes "into the house."

3. *Parallel Stories*. Biblical stories are sometimes designed to remind us of other narratives. This is achieved through parallelism, as when Jesus raises a widow's son (Luke 7) in a manner similar to that

of Elijah, or when Jacob is tricked into marrying the "wrong" daughter (Genesis 29), which recalls the way in which he tricked Isaac into blessing the "wrong" son.

4. *Placement of the Story.* Biblical stories are woven into the fabric of larger documents, and the narrator sometimes "aims" a story by its placement. In Mark 8, for example, a blind man is healed by Jesus with two touches. The first touch produces blurred vision, the second clarity. The story appears in the middle of another narrative, one about the disciples' gradual coming to clarity concerning Jesus' identity and the nature of his mission. The two stories are thus mutually informing. *"Bridge phrases,"* phrases such as "while he was still speaking," "after this," or "that same day," can sometimes provide clues to the interconnectedness of stories.

How in particular does the text under consideration, in its own literary setting, embody the characteristics and dynamics described in the previous questions?

How may the sermon, in a new setting, say and do what the text says and does in its setting?

In order to see how a preacher can move from a particular biblical narrative to a sermon on that narrative, let us take as our example Ruth 3:1-18. Because this text is a narrative episode which falls in the middle of a book best called a short story, both narrative types deserve comment.

A short story involves a comprehensive narrative design. The story consists of a beginning, a middle, and an end, and each small episode within plays a part in moving the larger plot toward resolution. If we examine the beginning of the Book of Ruth, we discover that the narrative is set in motion by the following developments:

1. The story is set during "the days when the judges ruled." Historical knowledge tells us this means it was "during the time when there was no *king.*"
2. We are told "there was a famine in the land," that is, "when there was no *food.*"
3. A man (Elimelech), his wife (Naomi), and their two sons (Mahlon and Chilion) migrated during the famine to Moab. There the man died. Then, the sons, after having married Moabite wives

(Orpah and Ruth), also died. Further developments make it plain that Naomi is too old to remarry and bear more sons, so we read this part of the story as "when there was no *son* to carry on the line of Elimelech."

4. Naomi plans to return to her home in Bethlehem and urges her daughters-in-law to remain in Moab so that they may remarry in their own land. Orpah does leave, but Ruth, in a moving and well-known scene, vows to remain with Naomi, saying, "Where you go I will go, and where you lodge I will lodge; your people shall be my people, and your God, my God" (1:16). This action is an important exception to the otherwise downward spiral of the plot.

5. Naomi and Ruth travel to Bethlehem and are greeted by the women of the town, who ask in startled wonder, "Is this Naomi?" Naomi refuses her own name, replying, "Do not call me Naomi, call me Mara [bitter], for the Almighty has dealt very bitterly with me. I went away full, and the Lord has brought me back empty." For this we can read "when Naomi had no *name* for the Lord had made her empty."

In summary, then, the Book of Ruth begins by presenting a family and its social setting, both of which are involved in a steady decline. In outline form, it looks like this:

No King
   ·
    ·
   No Food
      ·
       ·
      No Son
         ·
          ·
         No Name
            ·
             ·
            EMPTINESS

The exception in this descending pattern, the one glimmer of hope, is Ruth's action, loyally staying with Naomi when it would appear to be in her best interest to leave as Orpah did. This one action hints at and anticipates the coming ascent of the plot.

To appreciate the narrative design of the text, we must skip over the middle and examine the end. Ruth has married the landowner Boaz, a kinsman to Naomi who was introduced in the middle of the story, and they have had a son. Notice how the final scene (4:13–18) unfolds:

1. "The women said to Naomi, 'Blessed be the Lord.'" Naomi's *name* is restored.
2. The occasion for the women's blessing is that Naomi, through Ruth and Boaz, has been given a *son* and heir to the line of Elimelech.
3. Naomi herself places the newborn to her bosom and nurses him. She becomes, in her fullness, the provider of *food*.
4. The narrator provides a genealogy which indicates that this newborn son is to be the grandfather of David, the *king*.

Connecting beginning and end shows the overall movement of the plot.

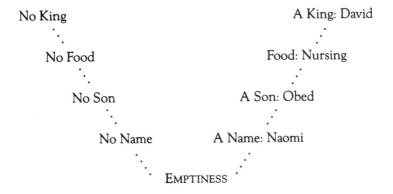

The double movement of the plot, downward and then upward, prompts the question, What happened in the middle of the story to create this transformation and to allow the end of the story to reverse the degeneration of the beginning?

The key to the resolution of the plot lay in the ancient law of Levirate marriage. The law (see Deut. 25:5–10) was intended to ensure that the line of a man who died with no heir would not be broken. If the law had been followed, a kinsman would have been obliged to marry into Elimelech's line and to father a son, thus maintaining the continuity of the family. Like many religious laws, however, this one was often more honored in the breech than in the practice. The next of kin to the Elimelech family is a man who appears in the story but remains nameless. We learn that he has no interest whatsoever in dusting off the law of Levirate marriage and fulfilling its obligations. However, Boaz, a wealthy landowner, is kin to the family of Elimelech as well, and we learn that he has developed more than a passing interest in the daughter-in-law, Ruth. Putting this together, Naomi plots a way out of the emptiness of her life. Since there is little chance that the next of kin, or Boaz, or anyone else for that matter, will fulfill the Levirate marriage provisions for purely religious reasons, she designs a means to provide a sexual motivation for doing so, thereby advancing the story. Naomi tells Ruth to make herself beautiful, to go to Boaz's barn, and, after Boaz has been satisfied with food and drink, to make herself available. "He will tell you what to do," promises Naomi. Ruth does almost everything that Naomi has told her to do, but not quite. She washes and puts on perfume. She goes to Boaz's threshing floor, and she waits until he has eaten and drunk. She even gives Boaz a subtle romantic signal, just as Naomi instructed her to do. Here, however, Naomi's scheme is altered in a surprising way. Instead of Boaz telling Ruth what to do, Ruth tells him, saying "Spread your skirt over your maidservant, for you are next of kin." Here is a Moabite peasant woman, an outsider with no status whatsoever, ordering a man of Israel to fulfill the ancient law of Israel's God. Boaz outmaneuvers the true next of kin and marries Ruth. He and Ruth not only provide a son to continue the line of Elimelech but become the great-grandparents of Israel's greatest king.

Preaching on this passage becomes an opportunity to forge a connection between the church and Boaz, to recall, through the inner workings of this story-within-a-story, how many times the people of God, the "insiders," have been called to covenant responsibility by "outsiders." Beyond the walls of every church lies a neighborhood, and a world—a Ruth, if you will—saying, "You are the next of kin.

Fulfill the Law." Every time a stranger—hungry, tired, broken in spirit, empty—appears at the door of the church the voice of Ruth is heard: "You are the next of kin. Fulfill the Law of God."

Preaching this passage also becomes an opportunity to speak a word of encouragement to those who seem themselves outside the community of faith. Naomi assumed that the insider would direct the outsider, but the story actually gives strength and purpose to the outsider. Sometimes, like Ruth, the outsider sees more clearly what the people of God are called to do, speaks more commandingly of the responsibilities God has placed before us. "You are the next of kin," Ruth said. "Fulfill the Law of God."

6
PREACHING
on the parables of Jesus

Preaching on a parable is a novice preacher's dream but often an experienced preacher's nightmare. The beginning preacher walks into a parable with a confident gait, striding boldly over what appears to be familiar terrain. Parables seem so much more accessible, more "preacher friendly," than many other types of Scripture. One may not have the faintest clue, for example, about the meaning of some opaque passage from Paul but Jesus' parables feel like comfortable territory. Rebellious sons leave home, farmers cast seeds, bridesmaids ready themselves for the wedding, pompous characters pray ostentatiously in church—these scenes from the parables appear to be both instantly recognizable and eminently preachable snapshots of human life.

But the more we get to know the parables, the less confident we become of our understanding of them. As soon as we reach out to grasp a parable's seemingly obvious truth, a trapdoor opens and we fall through to a deeper and unexpected level of understanding. Just as we are ready to play our interpretive hand, the parable deals us a new and surprising card, often making us unsure that we even know what game we are playing. The experienced preacher knows that the parables, so beguilingly simple on the surface, are, like a field with a hidden treasure, rich in meanings easily overlooked. Anyone who says from the pulpit, "What this parable means for us today," must speak in a cautious, humble, even trembling voice.

Luke tells us that just before Jesus told the parable of the Good Samaritan, he asked the lawyer, "How do you read?" That is precisely the question we must ask about the parables themselves. How do we read them? How should we approach a parable so that it can function *as* parable and yield to us its full depth of meaning?

Much depends, of course, upon what comes to mind when we think of the word "parable," since this implicit definition will govern the expectations we bring as readers. So, what *is* a parable? The parables of Jesus are popularly seen as masterful sermon illustrations, stories drawn from everyday life and designed to make difficult theological truths plain and easy to grasp—as the old saw has it, "earthly stories with heavenly meanings." According to this view, Jesus was a skillful teacher who employed parables to make his teachings clear, forceful, and memorable. If this is true, we should bring to the reading of a parable an expectation that we will be led firmly and lucidly to a deeper understanding of a theological idea.

While some of Jesus' parables do, in fact, seem to be "teaching stories" with self-contained theological lessons, not all of Jesus' parables fit neatly into this pattern. For example, the parable of the Unjust Steward (Luke 16:1-9), with its outrageous commendation of an apparent con artist, may be designed to teach a theological idea, but if so, crystal clarity is not one of this parable's virtues. Moreover, the only way many parables can be read as simple illustrations of single truths is by suppressing some of their more poetically engaging details. Some may wish to argue, for instance, that the parable of the Prodigal Son is an illustration of the one truth that God's love for sinners is boundless and endlessly patient. An average group of "naive" readers, however, will inevitably be "distracted" by other matters—what it meant for the younger son to "come to himself," the rivalry between the two brothers, and the justice of the father's treatment of the older son, for instance. The readers do not impose these matters on the parable; the parable itself stirs them up. The very texture of the parable, in other words, provokes in the reader a more complex process of discovery than merely comprehending a single, aptly illustrated idea.

In this light, some insist that Jesus' parables were intended not to make things clearer and easier for the hearer, but more difficult. Parables, they maintain, are mysterious sayings containing hidden, even secret, truths which must be "teased out" by the hearers. Perhaps they are even "narrative snares" designed, through their apparent ordinariness, to lull the hearers into complacency only to turn on them with a surprising and demanding twist of the plot. The problem with this view is its implication for our larger understanding of Jesus. Can we really imagine that Jesus' primary teaching device was intentionally obscure, as the troublesome passage Mark 4:10-12 seems to imply? According to Norman Perrin,

> Historically speaking, Jesus seems to have been one who was heard gladly and understood readily; the idea that his parables are esoteric and mysterious, needing a key to be understood, is foreign to everything we know about him. His parables are vivid, simple pictures, taken from real life.[1]

What, then, are the parables, and how do we read them? Should we read them as if they are panes of clear glass through which we "see" plainly, or as if they are multifaceted crystals which refract light in unexpected and enigmatic ways? How do we read?

The answer to this question, quite simply, is that the word "parable" is an elastic term which stretches to fit many different types of literature. Parables come in many shapes and do not all behave the same way rhetorically. There is no one way to read them; they require an unusual degree of flexibility on the reader's part. We must be prepared to begin reading a parable with one set of expectations, only to find that the parable resists and finally overthrows that expectation.

The remarkable diversity of the literary forms which are grouped under the label "parable" is evident when we examine a complete list of those passages which are typically called the "parables of Jesus." Some of Jesus' parables (e.g., the Prodigal Son [Luke 15:11-32]) are full-dress narratives with intricate plots and a rich cast of characters. Others (e.g., the Leaven [Matt. 13:33 and parallel] and the Fig Tree [Luke 13:6-9 and parallels]) are extremely brief, have but a single character or none, and have only the barest of plots, if they can be said to have plots at all. There are even instances in the New Testament of entirely non-narrative, maxim-like sayings of Jesus which are explicitly called parables (see, e.g., Mark 7:14-17).

When we look at the Semitic background of Jesus' use of parables, a background reflected in the Old Testament, the possibilities for understanding the diverse nature of parables become even greater. The Old Testament term *mashal* which corresponds to the New Testament *parabole* covers an array of verbal forms:

1. A commonly used saying that has its origin in a particular moment of history but has come to be widely applied to other events. In

1 Sam. 10:12 the question "Is Saul also among the prophets?" is called a *mashal*. (Cf. the modern inquiry, "Has he met his Waterloo?")

2. A human being who stands out as an example, usually in a negative sense. In Jer. 24:9 and Job 17:6, *mashal* (RSV, "byword") is not a saying but a negative description. Modern parallels would be our use of the name Hitler as a "byword" for evil and Machiavelli as a "parable" of political conniving.

3. A story that bears some similarity to the typical New Testament parable but is also clearly allegorical in intent. An example of this use of *mashal* is found in Ezek. 17:3–10.

Clearly, examples from both testaments show that parable is a difficult concept to define. The words *mashal* and *parabole* apply to many literary forms: maxims, ethical sayings, allegories, folk narratives, moral illustrations, and even exemplary persons. These diverse forms are obviously different in their rhetorical impact and demand distinct reading strategies. The real question is whether, in the face of this variety, it is meaningful to speak at all of a "parable genre." To say that a set of literary texts forms a genre implies that something holds them together, that at least at some level they can all be read in the same way. Parables, though, resist this understanding. Is there anything which binds together this assortment of literary expressions?

Many respond No to this question, maintaining that there are so many different brands of literature in the Bible that are called parable that the term itself is stretched out of useful critical shape. Their solution is to step outside the body of literature and supply a definition of parable derived from an external source—Aristotle, perhaps. Armed with this definition, they return to the texts which are "called" parables and separate the true parables (those which fit the definition) from the false ones.

An example of this in the history of parables interpretation involves the definition of parable which disallows allegory by insisting that a parable is unified around one central truth. Since allegory violates this unity by seeking to attach separate meanings to the various details of the text, parables cannot be allegories and allegories cannot be parables. The question now becomes, What does one do with texts such as Mark 12:1–11 (and parallels) that claim to be parables but also have clear allegorical implications? The choices are basically two: reject them as "false" parables or claim that they used to be "true" parables but were twisted into distorted, allegorical shape in the textual transmission process. The second option also allows for the use of scholarly tools to reconstruct the original parable, thereby freeing it from its allegorical mangling.

I am convinced, however, that much is lost when we force parables to jump through such a narrow definitional hoop. I want to suggest another approach, one that begins with the assumption that the biblical use of the terms *mashal* and *parabole* to cover a wide variety of verbal forms was neither careless nor accidental but reflective of the fact that these diverse forms share a common poetic root. They may demand a flexible reading strategy, but not an arbitrary one.

What holds these disparate verbal expressions together is their common capacity to generate two satisfactory levels of interpretation: the literal and the symbolic. A *mashal* or a *parabole* can be read both at face value and as representative of some deeper, less obvious, reality. This is true of virtually every biblical text which bears the parabolic label. The character Job, as a literary description of a human being, does not "stand for" anything other than himself. He is simply Job. When he describes himself as a *mashal*, though, he is saying that in addition to being Job the man he has become Job the symbol, representative of all that people find loathsome about human life. When the people saw the newly anointed Saul cavorting ecstatically with a roving band of prophets, they turned to each other and asked, "Is Saul also among the prophets?" There is nothing about this question that demands that we treat it symbolically. It can be taken at face value as a logical question arising out of a specific circumstance in Saul's life and nothing more. To call that question a *mashal*, though, indicates that it has the power to free itself from its original and literal place of reference. When a normally reserved professor suddenly rises in faculty meeting to make an impassioned, inspired, and charismatic speech, a surprised colleague may be moved to ask, "Is Saul also among the prophets?" The question has then become parabolic, pointing symbolically to all of those moments when the spirit seemingly has fallen upon an unlikely candidate. Likewise, when Jesus tells a story about a farmer sowing seed upon four different kinds of soil, it is possible to receive that narrative as an agricultural story and nothing more. To call it a parable, however, pushes us beyond its literal meaning, so that those who "have ears to hear" can apprehend its deeper meaning.

What we are saying here is more than the simple claim that a parable (including *mashal*) is symbolic. Rather parables of all sorts are *double entendres*, that is, they have both literal and symbolic references. One can always treat a parable literally and walk away with an interpretation which seems finished; but the parable also triggers in the reader an awareness that the literal word is not the last or the best word. One senses that dwelling longer with a parable offers the promise of discovering a second, symbolic level of meaning. Knowing this much, we are now ready to turn to the key questions.

What is the genre of the text?

As already noted, the term parable does not really describe a literary genre in the customary sense. Rather, it is a broad term which embraces certain kinds of narratives, proverbial sayings, literary figures, and popular slogans, all of which are grouped together under the label parable not because they share a common literary form but because they share an intrinsic capacity to be interpreted on both literal and symbolic levels.

Jokes, short stories, or newspaper articles tell us immediately what to expect and thus how to read them precisely because they *look* like jokes, short stories, or newspaper articles. Since parables come in many different forms, we must ask how readers intuitively recognize a parable when they see one. Some insight about this can come from examining C. H. Dodd's classic definition of a parable.

> At its simplest the parable is a metaphor or simile drawn from nature or common life, arresting the hearer by its vividness or strangeness, and leaving the mind in sufficient doubt about its precise application to tease it into active thought.[2]

Dodd clearly has his eye specifically on the parables of Jesus here, rather than on the whole body of parabolic literature, and that constricts his definition somewhat. Even so, he has come close to naming the essential characteristics of a parable. Two facets of Dodd's definition must claim our attention—the idea of parable as metaphor, and parable as vivid and strange communication.

1. When Dodd states that a parable is "a metaphor or simile" he is saying that a parable is symbolic communication, and he is specifying

two forms of the symbolic process: metaphor and simile. (See my discussion, below, of allegory, a symbolic form unfortunately not mentioned by Dodd.) Readers recognize a parable by virtue of the demand it somehow makes upon them to read at two levels simultaneously: the everyday, or literal, and the symbolic. Readers sense that while they may read a parable in a flat, non-interpretive manner, a part of the parable will then be lost to them.

How does a reader know to shift into symbolic gear when a parable is encountered? What is there about a parable which signals the reader to change reading strategies, to be alert to the symbolic value in the text? Sometimes the clue is straightforward: the author of the document in which the parable occurs will give us clues, phrases such as, "He proceeded to tell a parable." The narrator says, in not so many words, "Readers beware. Don't take this merely at face value." On other occasions, the fact that a parable seems out of place in the context in which it appears is the clue to its symbolic value. A story about a lost sheep told in the midst of a theological debate practically shouts at the reader to don the spectacles of symbol-interpretation.

On other occasions, though, something is odd about the parable itself; something within the parable cannot be taken literally. This leads to the second important aspect of Dodd's definition:

2. When Dodd claims that a parable "by its vividness or strangeness" leaves the reader uncertain of its meaning and, thus "teases" the reader into active thought, he is talking about the way in which the parable itself governs the process of reading.

Paul Ricoeur has given the name "extravagance" to this characteristic of parables. He points to those places in the parables which appear to be, as Dodd put it, "drawn from common life," but which are actually quite uncommon.[3] I suppose it is possible to imagine, for example, an employer paying the same wage to workers regardless of how long they worked during the day, or a host scouring the streets for banquet guests. Such actions are not completely out of the question, but they are decidedly eccentric. Likewise, while in everyday life seeds sprout and grow into plants, in the parables the smallest of all seeds produces a large shade tree filled with birds, and a few well-sown seeds yield a hundredfold harvest. Ordinariness is stretched to the breaking point, and the reader is almost forced to recognize that there is more here than meets the eye.

A parable, then, is a form of communication with two referents. Its first referent has to do with its literal, common, everyday meaning. But certain signals, internal or external, warn the reader not to be satisfied with the first referent and urge the reader to read on a symbolic level. To say that something is symbolic is like saying that something is music: it tells us what it is, but not how it works. Symbols function in many different ways, and parabolic symbols are no exception. In fact, this accounts for much of the diversity within the parables genre. (See below for a discussion of the symbolic process.)

Having examined the parables genre in broad terms, the focus of this section now narrows to include only the synoptic parables. Concern for the preaching of Jesus' parables immediately poses a critical question: Should we attend to the parables of Jesus as they are found in the Synoptic Gospels or should we attempt to recover the original spoken parables of Jesus? It is well known that Jesus' parables as they appear in the Gospels have the fingerprints of the early church all over them. Moreover, a number of scholars have produced persuasive reconstructions of what, in all probability, were the original oral parables. Joachim Jeremias, for example, in The Parables of Jesus, articulated ten ways in which the early church altered Jesus' parables. Jeremias claimed that the church often changed the audience of a parable, turned a parable into a hortatory device, or adjusted a parable to take account of new situations such as the delay of the Parousia. By identifying these tendencies, Jeremias in effect described the machinery by which the early church processed and transformed the original parables of Jesus. He then threw the machinery into reverse gear, inserted the synoptic parables, and out came plausible facsimiles of the original versions.[4] Much of Jeremias's work has been challenged and updated, of course, but a preacher who wishes to do so may reject the synoptic parables in favor of the originals and find abundant scholarly help in determining just what those originals were.

While this option is viable, I will here consider the parables as they appear in the canonical text. This does not mean that we must preach only those meanings which the Gospel writers highlighted in those parables, or that we will be blind to those places where alterations have clearly been made by the redactors. It does mean that the canonical texts, not hypothetically reconstructed originals, are the ones which we will explore homiletically.

What is the rhetorical function of this genre?

When the long history of parables interpretation is surveyed, three major images emerge which describe the ways in which people have understood the rhetorical functioning of Jesus' parables: the *code*, the *vessel*, and the *object of art*. These images are all built on the notion that Jesus' parables are symbols of the kingdom of God, but each contains a different assumption about how the symbolic process works.

The code was perhaps the earliest and certainly the most enduring way of understanding the parables. To view a parable as a code is to say that the parable symbolizes the kingdom of God allegorically (the one term missing from Dodd's list). When the parables are seen as codes, each important feature of a particular parable becomes a cipher for some unstated reality, and that parable can only be understood by those who have the knowledge necessary to "crack" it. Parables as code are only for the initiated, for those who have been given "the secret of the kingdom of God."

In the nineteenth century, the code concept was largely replaced by an understanding of parables as vessels, that is, as containers of concepts, general truths, or theological ideas. This development was more than a change in image; it was a change in the understanding of how the symbolic process works in the parables. Parables were no longer seen as allegories but as similes, as descriptions of everyday life which are *like* the kingdom of God in some illustrative way.

More recent students of the parables have replaced the vessel image with a view of the parables as objects of art. Like other art forms, parables are not pedagogical devices but aesthetic creations which engage readers in eventful encounter and invite new ways of seeing and understanding the human situation. The assumption underlying this approach is that parables are *metaphors* rather than allegories or similes, that is, they have the literary power to evoke an experience of the kingdom itself.

Rather than viewing these three images as competitive descriptions of the rhetorical function of parables, it is far more productive and truer to the literary range of the parables to see them as a set of possible strategies available to readers of parables. The set of synoptic parables contains examples of each rhetorical type. The reader, therefore, should approach a parable with the open question, Shall I read this as a code, as a vessel, as an object of art, or as some combination of these? The reader should then allow the parable itself to control the reading process and guide the reader toward the most apt strategy.

What does this mean in more practical terms? Let us examine the three types and their symbolic processes more closely.

Code

Some of the synoptic parables, if allowed to control the reading process, will lead us to read them as allegories. We will find ourselves saying things like, "The tenants represent Israel. The beloved son is Jesus," and so on. While we must be careful to avoid reading every parable this way, it is important to note that some parables are *constructed* as codes, and these parables themselves steer us in this direction.

It has been argued that the allegorical process is really foreign to the synoptic parables and that those parables which possess allegorical characteristics are either creations of the early church or severely distorted versions of Jesus' parables. In either case, it is alleged that the allegorical impulse is at war with the basic rhetorical drive of parables literature. On the other hand, Raymond Brown and Matthew Black, among others, have maintained that the distinction between parable and allegory was unknown to the ancient Semitic mind.[5] No one seriously contests the fact that both the early church and, especially, later exegetes drastically overinterpreted the allegorical aspect of the parables, but there is no clear reason to dismiss a more muted allegorical intentionality from the parables repertoire.

In technical terms, parables that are codes, that symbolize their nonliteral referent through the allegorical process, do so by matching each major aspect of the parable to a corresponding element in that deeper but hidden reality. So, $a = x$, $b = y$, $c = z$. Moreover, the relationship among a, b, and c inside the parable mirrors the relationship between x, y, and z outside.

While this is important, the more urgent question for a preacher is, What rhetorical impact does the code form have? What is it doing to the reader? In the main, codes affect readers in three significant ways. First, codes *confirm* what readers already know and believe.

Readers do not receive new information from allegorical texts; they have old information supported by receiving it in a new form. Second, codes *clarify* what readers already know and believe. If a reader who knows about the relationship between God and Israel "sees" that relationship in a story about a landlord and tenants, the nature of the relationship is clarified. Finally, codes *certify* the status of the readers as insiders. Outsiders receive the literal meaning of the coded parable; only an insider sees the full symbolic meaning. Reading a coded parable and being in the know certifies a person as one of the faithful.

Vessel

Other parables control the reading process by employing the dynamics of the simile. A simile is a figure of speech in which something we do not fully understand is said to be like something we do understand. "She is like a bird" is an example of a simile. Note, though, that this simile does not mean that she is like a bird in every way—she does not fly or eat worms; she is like a bird in one and only one respect—her spry personality, perhaps. The simile joins the known and the unknown at *one* juncture.

Parables that employ the dynamics of the simile are called vessels precisely because they point to one aspect of the deeper reality they symbolize. They are designed to embody a single truth. The rhetorical impact of the vessel parable is pedagogical: it teaches and illustrates that truth. If the reader of the code says, "Ah, yes, I know," the reader of the vessel says, "Aha, I see!"

Object of Art

There are still other parables that employ the dynamics of metaphor. If a simile says A is *like* B, a metaphor says A symbolically *is* B. Readers do not go to an object-of-art parable expecting to have what they already know about the kingdom of God confirmed or expecting to learn something about that kingdom. They go expecting to be drawn into the parable and to experience the claim of that kingdom itself. "The metaphor," states Perrin, "produces a shock to the imagination . . . which induces a new vision of world."[6] The reader of the object-of-art parable says neither, "Ah, yes, I know" nor "Aha, I see!" but rather, "Oh, my God, I never imagined."

Not every parable is pure code, vessel, or object of art. Some parables invite us to read them in more than one way. The parable of the Sower (Mark 4:1-9 and parallels), for example, obviously has a tradition of being read as a code, as evidenced by the allegorical interpretation given to it in the Gospels themselves (Mark 4:13-20 and parallels). This interpretation, though indisputably the creation of the early church, nevertheless has much to justify it as a true reflection of the rhetorical impact of the parable. But while it makes sense as a code, this same parable also invites us to read it as a vessel, containing the truth that despite the odds and the apparent forces of resistance God's eschatological harvest is sure and abundant. Moreover, if we allow this parable to cast us in the role of sower for the kingdom, the parable works metaphorically to create an experience of repeated failure followed by unexpected and gracious victory.

What literary devices does this genre employ to achieve its rhetorical effect?

Since most of the synoptic parables are narratives or quasi-narratives, much of what was said in chapter 5 concerning narrative in general applies to the parables as well. What concerns us here are those special features of parables which guide the reader toward reading the parable as code, vessel, or object of art.

In the code parable, there will usually be at least one detail which either does not comfortably fit the flow of the narrative or more aptly fits the outside reality symbolized by the parable than the situation within the parable. Matthew's version of the parable of the Marriage Feast (22:1-14), for example, tells of a king who gave a marriage banquet for his son. For some reason, when the meal was ready the invited guests refused to come. So what did the king do? "He sent his troops and destroyed those murderers and burned their city." Because this development is too bizarre to fit into the normal flow of the narrative the reading process is temporarily halted here. The reader's mind is tossed out of the narrative realm and into the world of history, since the detail in the parable clearly describes the historical destruction of Jerusalem better than it does anything that could occur at a wedding party. Once the reader has cracked one piece of the code by making this allegorical connection between the parable and history, he or she returns to the parable to read all of it in this light.

Parables are not always this obvious, of course. There is nothing in the parable of the Sower, for example, save the superabundant harvest, which would disrupt the reading process and eject us from the narrative world. In fact, it is read as code only because the seed's growth was patterned so closely to the early church's development that the parable "bled through" to its historical reality.

In a vessel parable, several devices are used to highlight the central truth being taught. Sometimes the parable is constructed to provide what is technically called "end stress," an emphasis upon the final episode and its implied meaning. A parable built in this way will typically have a series of episodes. In the first episode something happens; in the following episodes similar events occur. Only in the final episode does anything different happen, and this is where the rhetorical spotlight falls. The parable of the Good Samaritan is designed this way. A priest comes down the road, and passes by the man in the ditch. Next, a Levite comes down the road—and also passes him by. Only when the Samaritan arrives does the action change, and it is here we learn what it means to be a neighbor.

Another literary device employed in vessel parables is the language of comparison and contrast, often a clue that we are in the arena of simile. Note for instance the language of the parables in Luke 13:18-21:

> He said therefore, "What is the kingdom of God like? And to what shall I compare it? It is like a grain of mustard seed which a man took and sowed in his garden; and it grew and became a tree, and the birds of the air made nests in its branches."
> And again he said, "To what shall I compare the kingdom of God? It is like leaven which a woman took and hid in three measures of flour, till it was all leavened."

The language of comparison in these parables causes the reader to ask, "How is the kingdom like these things?" The reader searches through the parables for an answer. "Aha, I see," the reader says. "Though small and insignificant, the kingdom eventually becomes large and pervasive." With the question satisfactorily answered, the uncertainty of the two parables is resolved, and the truth contained in the vessels is disclosed.

In other parables, the synoptic redactor signals the reader to approach a parable as a vessel by the parable's placement or by the manner in which it is introduced. When the author of Matthew places the parable of Two Debtors (18:23–35) immediately after Peter's question about how often forgiveness should be given, he is signaling the reader to expect a lesson on forgiveness. When the author of Luke introduces the parable of the Unjust Judge (18:2–8) by saying, "And he told them a parable, to the effect that they ought always to pray and not lose heart," he is giving the reader not only a parable to look *at* but also a truth to look *for* in the parable.

Finally, some vessel parables express their core truths as formulas: "Watch therefore, for you know neither the day nor the hour," or "So the last will be first, and the first last." This is not to say that such parables contain *only* these stated truths or that they cannot be read as codes or objects of art as well, but that the redactors used these lines to underline these central ideas.

The object-of-art parable depends heavily upon one dynamic—the capacity to draw the reader into the world of the parable through identification with one of the characters of the parable or through a powerful set of images. The parable of the Good Samaritan has already served as an example of a vessel parable, but Robert Funk has described how it may also be read as object of art. "Initially, at least, the account compels the hearer to put himself in the place of that nameless fellow jogging along the wild and dangerous road."[7] Thus drawn into the parable as the unnamed man, the reader vicariously experiences the brutal attack of the robbers, the dashed hope and disillusionment as the priest and the Levite pass by, and ultimately the surprising—and in some ways unwelcome—ministry of the Samaritan's grace. The reader, Funk maintains, now a participant in the drama of the parable, is compelled to respond. "Is he willing to allow himself to be victim, to smile at the affront of the priest and Levite, to be served by an enemy?"[8]

Parables achieve this kind of identification by presenting a character in an open-ended way. The man going down the Jericho road, the son leaving home and demanding his inheritance, the servants who want to pull up the weeds in the field, or the older brother slavishly attending to his chores—we know enough about these and other parable characters to get a sense of them as specific people. Yet they are universal enough to recall our own experience. "In some ways, I'm just like that," we are likely to say.

In other object-of-art parables, the reader does not so much identify with one of the characters as with the world imaged in the parable. In the parable of the Laborers in the Vineyard (Matt. 20:1–16), readers may not see themselves as the vineyard owner or any of the workers, but they may become involved nonetheless in the world evoked by the parable. Readers may be led to wonder if the world, properly understood under the reign of God, is really built like the world of the parable, rather than the way the world seems on the surface. Which is real, the grasping, competitive world in which we live everyday, or the world of generosity created by the parable?

How in particular does the text under consideration, in its own literary setting, embody the characteristics and dynamics described in the previous questions?

How may the sermon, in a new setting, say and do what the text says and does in its setting?

In v. 1 of the parable of the Wicked Tenants (Mark 12:1–11), Mark announces that what follows is a parable, thereby signaling the need for a symbolic reading. But what are we to look for? Is this parable a code, a vessel, or an object of art? We do not yet know, and we must be prepared to let the parable tell us how to read.

We do not have to wait very long before we receive our first clue: "A man planted a vineyard." We pause and explore the image of vineyard. Old Testament vineyards, perhaps especially the one in Isaiah 5, come to mind. Is this where we belong? We return to the parable: "And set a hedge around it, and dug a pit for the wine press, and built a tower." Now there can be no question. This is surely the language of Isaiah. The parable has thrown us out of its own world and into the story of God and Israel.

This parable is a code; and once the reader begins to expect this from the parable, other pieces fall into place. As John Drury outlines it, "The 'man' is God, the vineyard Israel, the tenants Jews or Jewish authorities. All that is known from Isaiah 5. The servants are Old Testament worthies and prophets, often called such in the Old

Testament."[9] As the scenes of violence, shame, and emptiness unfold, the reader recognizes their Old Testament parallels and makes
the allegorical connections.

As the reader follows the narrative, however, a new element is
suddenly encountered: "He had still one other, a beloved son." Once
again the reader is ejected from the parable, this time to land not in
the Old Testament but in the larger framework of Mark itself. "Thou
art my beloved Son," proclaimed the heavenly voice at the baptism of
Jesus (1:11). The reader knows both the identity and the fate of the
"beloved son" because Mark has already disclosed it: "The Son of
man must suffer . . . and be rejected . . . and be killed" (8:31). It is
no surprise for the reader, then, to find that the tragedy of the
parable unfolds in just that way.

It is not difficult to decipher the code. But what is the rhetorical
impact of the parable? First, the parable confirms what the reader
already knows and thereby certifies the insider status of the reader.
The reader has encountered a familiar historical story recast in a new
parabolic form and thus says, "Not everyone would know what this
story is really about, but I do." This calls the reader, in effect, to a
confession of faith. "Who am I?" wonders the reader. "I am a person
who knows the story behind the story. I am a person who can recite
the ways in which God's people have rejected God with violence,
even the beloved Son."

The parable does more, however, than call the familiar story to
mind. It provides the reader with clarity. By retelling the familiar in a
new way, aspects of what the reader has always known come into
sharper view. The parable asks, What will the owner of the vineyard
do? The servants have all been killed. Even the beloved son has been
killed. What will the owner of the vineyard do? Will he abandon the
vineyard? No. He will come and destroy the tenants, and give the
vineyard to others. The reader has known this, too, but now sees it
with greater clarity, and is both comforted and warned. The comfort
lies in knowing that not even rejection by God's people can stop God
from tending the vineyard, the warning in realizing that if the people
of God will not care for it, the vineyard will be given to the care of
others. Thus the reader is prepared for the ending of the Gospel
where Mark will tell the reader that at the crucifixion one of those

"others," a gentile centurion, stood in the vineyard and cried, "Truly this man was the Son of God" (15:39).

The parable thus puts us as readers in an interesting and ambiguous role. As members of the Christian community we are historically and allegorically the "others" in the parable, those to whom the vineyard will be given. As insiders to the parable's code, however, we are the new tenants, now entrusted with the stewardship of the vineyard.

What can a sermon on this parable do to extend the power of the parable into the life of a congregation? First, the parable should be read or perhaps even retold with dramatic sensitivity. The congregation will almost surely begin to recognize or remember the linkages between the parable and the Christian story. The preacher may then want to strengthen those connections, recalling moments in ancient and modern history when the action of God in the world has been rejected by the very ones called to cherish it. This part of the sermon becomes a kind of confession of faith and of sin, an acknowledgment that the words "suffered under Pontius Pilate, crucified, dead, and buried" reflect a constant theme in the interaction between God and the world. The sermon may then move to both the comfort and the warning of the parable. We are assured that God has not abandoned the world but is still at work cultivating the vineyard. We are, however, called to wonder what kind of tenants we are. Are we the kind who do violence to God's work, or are we the kind who are able to say, "The very stone which the builders rejected has become the head of the corner; this was the Lord's doing and it is marvelous in our eyes."

Let us now explore a different sort of parable, actually a pair of parables: The parable of the Hidden Treasure and the parable of the Pearl (Matt. 13:44–46) are a pair of parables that function as a unit. They appear in the middle of Matthew 13, which is itself a collection of parables. Matthean scholars have long observed that Matthew 13 forms a turning point in the flow of the Gospel. Jack Dean Kingsbury notes that through chapter 12 Matthew has described a ministry of Jesus to the Jews, which has been rejected on all sides. Now Jesus turns to the disciples as the true people of God, and, according to

Kingsbury, it is "Jesus' turning away from the Jews and towards his disciples . . . [that] is meant by the great 'turning point.'"[10]

The two parables, then, appear in Matthew just at the point when Jesus turns his attention from one audience to another. It is significant that while the first twelve chapters of Matthew include images, metaphors, and other parable-like elements, there is no actual use of the word "parable" until the beginning of chapter 13 (13:3). In the economy of Matthew's Gospel, parables are a "post-turning point" form, intended only for the disciples, the new Israel.

When careful readers of Matthew's Gospel come across this new term "parable," they are immediately aware that they have entered new linguistic territory. They are invited to begin reading in a new and symbolic way and are thus initiated into the inner circle. The reader joins those to whom "it has been given to know the secrets of the kingdom of heaven" (13:11).

What happens to readers when they encounter the two parables in question? The first line tells them that "the kingdom of heaven is like treasure hidden in a field." The word "hidden" momentarily disrupts the reading process, sending the reader back a dozen verses to the parable of the Leaven (13:33), in which the kingdom was also said to be like something hidden. Since the reader is thrown not into the world of history but into another parable, and since both parables are controlled by the language of simile ("the kingdom of heaven is like . . ."), the reader is led toward reading the parable as a vessel. The kingdom is like leaven and the kingdom is like a buried treasure, that is, hidden, waiting to be revealed. The readers are guessing at this point, but the best guess seems to be that the two parables are vessels containing the same theological content.

But then, something happens which makes the reader guess again. The reader encounters yet another parable, one unmistakably connected to the treasure parable by the word "again." The two parables are meant to be read together, but this time nothing is hidden. A merchant is searching for fine pearls, and fine pearls are difficult to find, to be sure, but they are not hidden from view. This development causes the reader to feel uncertain, since the expected approach to reading the parable is now not possible. These two parables will not reduce to a common theological concept.

So the reader must reread the first parable and compare it to the second. What holds these two episodes together? John Dominic Crossan has observed that what makes the two parables a pair is the sequence of verbs: finds, sells, buys. The parables are matched not because they are vessels which contain the same *idea* but because they are brief narratives which share the same essential *plot*. The parables, clearly, are not vessels; they demand to be read as objects of art. It is the plots which draw the readers into the world of the two parables. As Crossan observes, in both parables someone's projected future is suddenly shattered by the advent of a new event, by something which is found. In the force of this advent, the person willingly reverses the past, "selling all that he has," and receives a new world of action he did not have before.[11] Finding–selling–buying . . . advent–reversal–action—this is the world to which these parables invite the readers.

The primary task of a sermon on these parables is not, then, to explain anything but to evoke the world of kingdom advent–reversal–action beckoned by the texts. The sermon may begin by exploring moments in human life, be they searched for or stumbled over, which possess this dynamic: the birth of a baby, a word of comfort spoken in a time of crisis, the letter we have been waiting for or didn't expect, the reaction of the adopted child who has discovered the identity of her natural parents, the encounter of a human need so close and so dire that we can not turn numbly away from it. These are advent–reversal–action moments.

The sermon cannot remain at this level, however. Jesus' stories are parables of the kingdom, and the sermon must finally name the theological depths. Where are those moments when we experience the advent of God's grace, and are thereby freed to give up what we had previously cherished and opened up to a new and unexpected world of action?

Dan Wakefield, writing in *The New York Times Magazine*, described his own experience of religious reawakening.[12] In the midst of a year of extreme stress during which Wakefield, a writer, lost both of his parents, left his job, ran out of money, and saw an important relationship with a woman dissolve, he "one day grabbed an old Bible . . . , and with a desperate instinct turned to the Twenty-third Psalm." Reading the psalm did not result in a miraculous breakthrough. "It simply seemed an isolated source of solace and calm," he wrote, It was, however, the first glint of the pearl, the initial knocking of the plow blade as it struck something hidden beneath the furrow.

This experience and others gradually led Wakefield back into the community of faith. "I experienced," he reported, "a feeling simply and best described as a 'thirst' for spiritual understanding and contact; to put it bluntly, I guess, for God." Slowly he became liberated from what he called the "life numbing addictions" of alcohol and drugs:

> At some point or other they felt as if they were "lifted," taken away, and instead of having to exercise iron control to resist them, it simply felt better not to have to do them anymore. The only concept I know to describe such an experience is that of "grace," and the accompanying adjective "amazing" comes to mind along with it.[13]

When the merchant found the pearl of great value, he "went and sold all that he had and bought it." Advent-reversal-action: such is the world of these parables.

7
PREACHING
on epistles

Even though in its preaching and liturgy the church has tended to place its greatest emphasis upon the four Gospels, the epistle is the "dominant literary form found within the Christian canon."[1] At least twenty of the twenty-seven books in the New Testament present themselves as letters, and two other books include material in epistolary form (Acts 15:23-29; 23:26-30; Revelation 2—3). So useful and influential was the epistle form that it continued to prevail in the period of the Apostolic Fathers.[2] If it is true that the identity of the church's Lord was disclosed most clearly in the Gospels, it is also the case that the character of the church's life was shaped most tangibly by the letter.

What is the genre of the text?

For centuries the letter has been the most common form of written communication. While not everyone writes poems, songs, essays, or books, virtually every literate person writes letters. Letters can be formal (Dear Ms. Smith, I am writing to apply for the position of sales representative . . .) or informal (Dear Sarah, Where did the summer go? It seems like a year since we were walking together on the beach . . .). They can plead a cause (I encourage your vote against the current agriculture bill), register a complaint (I am very disappointed in the performance of my new quartz watch), provide information (The weather here has been cold and rainy for two weeks), issue an invitation (Can you and Jim spend the weekend with us?), state an opinion (Your recent editorial completely obscured the central issue), or express an emotion (I love you more every day). They can be addressed to individuals (Dear Larry) or to groups (Dear Committee Members). In every case, though, a letter involves someone saying something to someone else in the context of a specific situation.

In this sense, true letters (as opposed to "open letter" essays, epistolary novels, and other types of literature which assume the letter format but are not actual correspondence) are the closest literary form to oral conversation. Letters have a dialogical flavor. When we read a letter, we can almost hear the inflections of the writer's voice, speaking about something to someone else, whose presence we can also feel. Look at the following excerpt from a letter:

Dear Rob,
    You guessed it would be a boy, and you were right! On Monday at 3:16 A.M., Janice and I became the proud parents of Samuel Thompson Miller—all nine pounds, six ounces of him! The picture was taken yesterday. Don't you think he has Janice's chin?

Even though we do not know the people named in this letter, we have a sense about them. A little bit of the personalities of both the writer and recipient are revealed through the letter, as is something of the situation from which the letter arises. This is why reading someone else's personal mail, like eavesdropping, is an invasion of privacy.

We can see these personal and immediate characteristics even in those letters which we know are impersonal and general, such as the computer-generated letter which begins, "Dear Mr. Roth, Because of your outstanding credit record you are one of the very few selected to receive our prestigious Gold Card." The idea is to make Mr. Roth feel as though someone *knows* him, has been watching approvingly as he faithfully paid his bills, and, having noticed him, now *trusts* him.

It is important to note that even though letters can approximate oral conversation, they are not the same thing as oral conversation. Television commercials tout long distance telephone calls as "the next best thing to being there," implying that if you can't actually be with another person, you can, as a good second choice, achieve a similar closeness through a telephone call. It is a mistake, however, to think of letters as an earlier version of "the next best thing to being there." William Doty's claim that the "Pauline letters were at best a makeshift substitute for Paul's presence with the addressees"[3] may be accurate in terms of Paul's psychological intent but is rhetorically off the mark. Letters are another—and different—way of being there. To put it more accurately, letters are a way of "being there" and "not being there" at the same time. They are a unique blend of closeness and distance.

Suppose, for example, a woman wakes up on the morning of her twentieth wedding anniversary to find on her dressing table a letter from her husband, in the form of an anniversary card. He has departed for the day, but there is the card. It contains the kind of printed thought typical of such cards, and a brief note of affection written and signed by her husband. As in a personal conversation, the husband, the wife, and their immediate circumstances are implicit in that card. There is closeness, but there is distance as well. The husband could have *said*, directly and orally, everything the card says; its impact in a card—a letter—is somehow different.[4] The card is not a "makeshift substitute" for oral, face-to-face conversation. It blends many of the qualities of personal presence with the reality of absence.

There is another difference between letters and oral conversation. Conversations are apt to be fleeting, tied to the moment in which they are uttered. Letters, precisely because they are written, tend toward a more lasting quality. Since time necessarily passes between the composition and the reading of a letter, and since letters are actually "written," they, unlike most conversation, possess a capacity for transcending a single time and place.

Imagine that a missionary couple on furlough spends a weekend with one of the local congregations providing their support. Upon returning to their mission station, they write a personal letter to the pastor, thanking him for the hospitality extended to them and informing him of what has happened to them since their return to their place of ministry. The pastor, knowing that the congregation would be interested in the letter, posts it on the church bulletin board. For several weeks, members of the congregation pause in the hallway to read the letter. Some read it on more than one occasion, finding new meaning in it each time. Finally the letter is taken down from the board and given to the local church historian who will include it in an informal history of the church she is writing. What began as a personal letter has become in effect a "general epistle." It still evokes the immediate circumstances of its composition, but it also speaks beyond them.

The same is true, of course, for the letters included in the New Testament. These epistles, for the most part, were originally directed at a particular set of circumstances in a congregation's life but through the process which led eventually to canonization were posted on the "bulletin board" of the whole church. Early New Testament scholars, Adolf Deissmann for example, attempted to distinguish between *letters* and *epistles*. Epistles, they argued, are more formal, essay-like documents intended for a general, nonspecific audience, while *letters* like Paul's are spontaneous, unaffected expressions bound to specific and individual situations. More recent scholarship has moved away from this sharp definitional dichotomy. Paul's letters, the prime examples of New Testament epistles, are now viewed, in a more balanced manner, both as documents directed at particular circumstances in the early church and, by their very character as letters, as material which possesses implications and has the capacity to endure beyond the immediate situation. Moreover, even though Paul's letters contain many personal, specific, and even fleeting personal references, it is clear that most were composed to be read to the whole worshiping congregation, perhaps over and over again (see, e.g., 1 Thess. 5:27). In short, the letters of the New Testament are like almost all other letters: connected to a specific set of circumstances but inherently capable of speaking beyond those immediate conditions.[5]

Another characteristic of letters is their stylized format. Consider what happens when a person sits down to write a letter. Without much forethought or planning, the writer follows a conventional set of compositional "rules." Letters begin in certain ways, end in certain ways, and are even arranged on the page in standard patterns with only slight variations of the basic format depending upon the type of letter. The writer is free, of course, to violate these conventions, but a change in the formula will inevitably create a rhetorical effect different from the normal letter's. A formal letter to the President of the United States could begin casually, "Hey Prez," but it would be immediately apparent that the accepted form had been abandoned.

While letters in the New Testament generally follow the accepted patterns of letters in the ancient world, they modify the rules a bit. Such changes were often due to the fact that these letters were shaped by the content and character of the Christian faith. William Doty has argued persuasively that the apostle Paul gradually adapted the typical Greco-Roman model of the letter for Christian purposes, thereby creating a new literary genre which strongly influenced subsequent Christian letter writing. He writes,

> I argue that there is a basic understanding of structure by which Paul wrote, but that this basic understanding could be modified on occasion, and that the basic understanding came into being only gradually. I am not as concerned to argue the case for developmental stages in Pauline thought or literary concept as to convince the reader that when he reads Pauline correspondence, he is witnessing the creation of a genre which was to have an impressive afterlife. Certain post-Pauline letters revert to more orthodox Hellenistic letter models; others slavishly imitate Paul. But at no time after the writing and publication of the Pauline letters were early Christian writers able to ignore the impact of the Pauline letters. They were the model for early Christian literature in ways that the gospels and histories could not be, and the line of generic contact continued from Paul down through the encyclicals and papal letters of subsequent generations.[6]

What is the rhetorical function of this genre?

Entering a New Testament letter is like exploring a large house in which each room has been decorated by a different designer. The architecture, it is true, has an overall impact but each room has its own aesthetic. Similarly, it is possible to speak about the rhetorical function of a letter as a whole—how its various elements are arranged, the sort of reading expectations it sets up—but it is also important to consider the rhetorical function of the several sections of that same letter. A typical letter, constructed in conventional fashion, may contain narrative, dialogue, direct address, formal argument, or poetry, each with its own rhetorical rules and effects. Indeed, one of the characteristics of a letter is that it alerts the reader to the need to respond quickly to changing rhetorical signals, to switch reading strategies from paragraph to paragraph.

Before we can appreciate how the smaller units in a letter function, we need to draw back and survey the whole. What does a New Testament letter, in the largest sense, "do" for and with its readers? We can begin to answer this question by looking at the literary characteristics of the Greek letter, the type of correspondence that served as a blueprint for the New Testament letters. Heikki Koskenniemi has identified three primary rhetorical functions of the typical Greek letter.[7]

1. *Philophronesis.* The evocation and expression of a "friendly relationship" between the writer and the recipient. Modern phrases (e.g., "Dear Fred," and "Sincerely yours,") retain this rhetorical intuition that letters are to be read in the context of a cordial, trusting relationship.

2. *Parousia.* The establishment of "presence," the sense that the purpose of the letter is to bridge the gap of physical separation between writer and reader. A letter did not merely relay information between two parties; it brought something of the sender into contact with the recipient. This quality is retained in modern letter writing: the excitement we often feel when we find a letter from a loved one in the mailbox comes not just from an anticipation of the information we will read in the letter but also from an awareness of the presence of the person in the letter.

3. *Omilia* and *Dialogos.* The creation of a dialogical, invitational mood of homily and dialogue similar to the tone of Greek letters. Letters had something to say, and they said it dialogically, that is, in an attempt to include the reader, and with the reader's attitudes and feelings in mind. Again, an examination of modern letters discloses these same qualities. "As I am sure you will remember"; "This may be hard for you to believe, but"; "Please forgive my delay in answering" all indicate that, like their models, contemporary letters convey their content in dialogical fashion.

How do New Testament letters, especially Paul's, fit into this rhetorical scheme? *Philophronesis*, the friendly relationship between Paul and his readers, is evident, but it has become significantly nuanced by the Christian faith. Whereas in Greek letters, the friendship between the two parties had no referent other than itself, Paul's relationship to his letters' recipients usually points beyond itself to their common relationship in Christ. In Paul's hands, the customary Greek salutation, *chairein* (greeting!), becomes *charis* (grace), with its attendant theological freight. The friendly relationship becomes one of "partnership in the gospel" (Phil. 1:5) and of "boasting of you in the churches of God for your steadfastness and faith" (2 Thess. 1:4).

As William Doty has observed,

> While there are many times when the Pauline letters do function to
> maintain friendly relationships, their purpose goes beyond that; Paul
> sought to bring his addressees into richer experiences of the new reli-
> gion, to move them to new heights of action and response, not merely
> to improve or maintain relationships to himself.[8]

Parousia or presence is clearly a characteristic in Pauline correspondence. This is not a simple or clear issue, however, since letters,
as we have noted, combine a certain kind of presence with actual absence. This dynamic is clearly evident in 2 Corinthians 10, which
begins:

> I, Paul, myself
> entreat you, by the meekness and gentleness of Christ—
> I, who am humble when face to face with you,
>   but bold to you when I am away!—
> I beg of you that when I am present I may
>   not have to show boldness with such
>   confidence as I count on showing
>   against some who suspect us of acting
>   in worldly fashion.
>   (vv. 1–2)

The powerful and repeated language of presence begins with the
intensifying triplet "I . . . Paul . . . myself." These are not merely
Paul's ideas in this letter. Paul, the person, is present and speaking.

Yet there is a difference between Paul's physical presence and
his presence in the letter. Paul himself acknowledges this when he
indicates, quoting, with irony, his opponents, that in the flesh he is
"humble," but in the letter he is "bold." Indeed, this distinction
between Paul "in person" and Paul the correspondent had evidently
been a matter of discussion in Corinth, since later in the chapter
Paul quotes some of his local critics to that effect:

> For they say,
> "His letters are weighty and strong,
> but his bodily presence is weak,
>   and his speech of no account."
>   (10:10)

The historical circumstances behind this charge are a matter of
conjecture, but the basic situation is clear. Paul's personality and

authority have been experienced differently by the Corinthians in his writing than in his personal visits, and his opponents have seized upon this difference and turned it into an accusation of duplicity. The forceful Paul of the letters, they say, is a sham; the real Paul is a weakling. Paul responds:

> Let such people understand
> that what we say by letter when absent,
> we do when present.

In other words, Paul argues that the Paul who speaks and is present in the letters is the same Paul who visits them in person. There is continuity between the words of the man in the letters and the actions of the man in the flesh.

So we have a very interesting debate going on in Corinth. Will the real Apostle Paul please stand up? Is the Apostle Paul the iron-man the Corinthians have experienced in the letters, or the less impressive flesh-and-blood human being who visited them? Paul argues continuity; his critics argue fraud. Who is right?

The nod goes, of course, to Paul, but when we look at this conflict through the lens of literary dynamics, the grounds upon which his opponents were able to make their case are apparent. Letters—at least truthful ones—enable the writer to be present to the reader. This was Paul's point. But in a letter, the writer is present in a different way than in face-to-face communication. It was this difference, inherent in the letter form, which Paul's opponents manipulated into a charge of duplicity. While it may seem at first that this quality puts the letter at a communicational disadvantage, and while it is true that a letter imposes limits upon a personal encounter that are not present in oral conversation, a letter grants a certain freedom as well.

In order to grasp both the difference between a letter and face-to-face conversation and the potential freedom afforded by a letter, imagine that a father has just received a copy of his son's first-quarter college grades and is very displeased. His son, it appears, has spent more time trying to make it in a fraternity than in physics, literature, and political science. The father considers three options for expressing his displeasure. He can drive the three hundred miles to the university and give his son a piece of his mind. He can telephone his son and make essentially the same speech. Or he can write his son a letter stating his anger and disappointment.

These may appear to be relatively equal means for conveying an unpleasant message until they are analyzed from the son's point of view. If his father suddenly shows up, unannounced, in his dormitory room blowing steam, the stakes will be high. Every charge must be answered on the spot, because there will be this parent pacing around the room, thrusting his arms into the air, and demanding a response. It will be a raw and full encounter between two human beings which may end in alienation, or it may end in an embrace. If the father chooses the telephone to make his speech, the threat is perhaps reduced a bit by the distance, but the exchange will still be immediate and direct, and the dynamics will be essentially those of the face-to-face encounter.

If, however, the father sends a letter, there is a significant shift in the dynamics. The son will certainly experience, in the emotion-laden language of the letter, his father's presence, but not the full range of that presence. The letter will bring only part of the father's person into focus. Moreover, once the letter has been written, it is fixed. Unlike the father's spoken words, the letter's can neither soften nor become further inflamed. At the same time, the letter affords the son the time and distance necessary to recover from the shock, think through the problem, and plan a response. The letter both renders the father present and protects the son from the full demand of that presence. Out of this simultaneous presence and absence arises a certain amount of freedom for both the writer and recipient.

The writers of letters are free to express themselves more energetically, plainly, and forcefully in letters than they might in oral conversation. There are some things that are "easier to put in a letter." Why is it that we can often express our love, our rage, or our care for one another better in a letter than we can face-to-face? Because a letter is a way of genuinely being present to another person without the risk of being fully present.

The readers of letters are free to reject a letter without having to reject a person. This freedom pushes the letter rhetorically toward what Koskenniemi calls *dialogos*. In personal conversation, we can press our claims through the forcefulness of personality, but a letter, no matter how vigorously phrased, must finally be invitational and dialogical to be persuasive. We can see this dialogical element in many Pauline phrases:

> Do you not know, brethren—for I am speaking to those who know the law—that the law is binding on a person only during his life? (Rom. 7:1)
>
> Now I would remind you, brethren, in what terms I preached to you the gospel. (1 Cor. 15:1)
>
> Are we beginning to commend ourselves again? Or do we need, as some do, letters of recommendation to you, or from you? (2 Cor. 3:1)
>
> Open your hearts to us; we have wronged no one. (2 Cor. 7:2)
>
> Let me ask you only this: Did you receive the Spirit by works of the law, or by hearing with faith? (Gal. 3:2)
>
> And I ask you also, true yokefellow, help these women. (Phil. 4:3)
>
> But as to the times and the seasons, brethren, you have no need to have anything written to you. For you yourselves know well that the day of the Lord will come like a thief in the night. (1 Thess. 5:1-2)

In each case, although Paul is the writer, the reader's voice is invoked. This dialogical quality is important to the letter form in general, but in the New Testament epistles it is also undergirded by theological and ecclesiological considerations. William Doty says,

> I would argue that the epistle remained a viable and popular genre within early Christianity precisely because "it worked" to meet cultural needs. The epistle was just the form of language act necessary to the exploratory expansion of the primitive Christian movement. Letters of the Pauline sort did not function primarily to set out dogmas and locked-in theological criteria of faith. To be sure, these letters were not noncommittal! They certainly expressed Paul's position on important religious issues, and sometimes they were too ethos-reflecting to suit our sophisticated tastes (Paul's low view of women, for example). But integral to the movement of the letters is a dialogic quality, a willingness to be addressed by the religious perspectives one was recalling.[9]

What literary devices does this genre employ to achieve its rhetorical effect?

Letter writers, ancient and modern, have been aware of the "rules" for constructing a proper letter. The address goes here, the signature goes there, and so on. Even though the writers of the New Testament letters made theologically guided changes in those rules, there is still an identifiable "standard form" for the New Testament epistle. Since passages from the epistles possess meaning not only by virtue of their immediate content but also through their placement within the framework of this customary letter form, preachers need to "know their way around" the typical form of a New Testament letter—the opening, the thanksgiving, the body, and the closing.

Opening

New Testament letters customarily begin first with an identification of the writer, then an identification of the recipients, and finally a theological greeting.

In modern letters, the writer is identified at the *end* of the letter. Rarely do we read a letter, though, without peeking at the signature or the return address so that we will know from the outset who is writing to us. Writers in the first century A.D., however, were more logical. Even though there may have been a handwritten signature at the end (see 2 Thess. 3:17, for example), they customarily identified themselves in the opening line of their letters.

Regardless of where it is located, the form a letter writer's self-identification takes is a clue to the character of the letter. Consider the ways in which the same person may identify herself in a variety of letters:

Sincerely yours,	Cordially,
Barbara D. Mercer	Barb
President and CEO	
Mercer Graphics, Inc.	
Love,	Sincerely,
Babs	Barbara (Dennison) Mercer
	Class Agent
	Class of '58

In each case, we immediately know something about both the nature of the letter and the relationship between the writer and the recipient. In similar fashion, the preacher can learn much by paying attention to the identification sections of the New Testament epistles.

Compare, for example, the way Paul identifies himself to the Philippians ("Paul and Timothy, slaves of Jesus Christ") to the way he identifies himself to the Galatians ("Paul, an apostle—not from humanity
nor through human agency, but through Jesus Christ and God
the Father, who raised him from the dead"). In Philippians, the humility that will become a theme in the letter is already apparent. In
Galatians, however, the aggrieved apostle, whose standing and authority have been challenged, is in the ring from the outset, sparring
with his opponents.

It is also instructive to explore the ways in which recipients are
identified. Receiving a letter that begins, "To the Members of the
Department of Practical Theology," I ready myself for a certain kind
of reading experience. One that opens, "Dear Taxpayer," prepares
me for another kind of experience. "Dear Reverend Long," "Dear
Tom," and "My Dearest Tom" each summon forth different parts of
me and focus my anticipation in different ways on what is to follow.
In his letters Paul identifies his recipients in a variety of ways: "God's
beloved . . . called to be saints" (Romans); "called to be saints together with all those who in every place call on the name of our
Lord" (1 Corinthians); "the church . . . in God our Father and the
Lord Jesus Christ" (1 and 2 Thessalonians); "our beloved fellow
worker" (Philemon); or—getting down to brass tacks—just plain
"the churches of Galatia."

The final element in the opening of a New Testament letter is the
greeting. The typical greeting of a Pauline letter is "Grace to you and
peace from God our Father and the Lord Jesus Christ." "Grace," as
we have noted, is almost surely a theological extension of the classic
Greek "greetings"; "peace" (shalom) is the traditional opening of Jewish letters. This use of shalom connects the Christian epistle, primarily Hellenistic in form, to the Jewish theological tradition.[10]

Thanksgiving

After the opening section, Pauline letters characteristically move to
a thanksgiving, a characteristic of Greek letters which Paul adapts
to his theological purposes. These sections are, strictly speaking,
prayers, an important fact when considering their rhetorical effect.
Paul, in effect, begins his letters by saying, "Hello. This letter is from
Paul, but before we begin, let us pray." And then for a paragraph (or,

in the case of 1 Thessalonians, for three chapters), the reader pauses while Paul prays. He directly addresses God, not the reader. The reader "overhears" the prayer, though; and Paul, who is quite aware of this dynamic, uses the prayer to anticipate the contents of the letter. In 1 Corinthians, for example, Paul, who will later address in detail the problems of speaking in tongues, idle talk in worship, and conflict over spiritual gifts, thanks God "that in every way you were enriched in all speech and knowledge . . . so that you are not lacking in any spiritual gift" (1 Cor. 1:5, 7). In Philemon, Paul appeals for Philemon to receive Onesimus, his runaway slave, as a Christian brother, praying, "I thank my God always . . . because I hear of your love and of the faith which you have toward all the saints." Paul speaks to God, but his eye is also on Philemon, who will be asked to show faith once again toward a controversial saint. In the same way that liturgical eucharistic prayers are brief summaries of Christian convictions, Paul's eucharistic prayers are shorthand summaries of the theological and practical matters that will follow.

It is significant that among the Pauline letters only Galatians contains no thanksgiving section. Evidently Paul, like an angry modern correspondent who purposefully omits the "Dear" from the salutation, intended that his readers notice his departure from the customary form, feel the consequent emotional impact, and think, "There is nothing about us for which he can give thanks."

Body, including Paraenesis

Paul now rises from prayer to address his readers. This, the main section of the letter, usually includes discussions of the crucial matters at hand—the body—and practical ethical matters—the paraenesis. George A. Kennedy has applied the categories of classical rhetoric to the Pauline epistles and found that Paul often developed his thought according to the formal patterns of well-known rhetorical "types."[11] A knowledge of such classical rhetorical styles will help the preacher recover the way in which the text achieves its effect, especially when the technique is unfamiliar. In general, though, information about the detailed structures of formal argument is simply a specialized aid for the more general task of allowing one's expectations and reading of the text to be guided by the rhetorical cues it contains.

One technical rhetorical device employed in the letters of the New

Testament, the *chiasmus*, deserves special attention both because it is used so frequently and because it is easily missed by the contemporary reader. The chiasmus was a way of speaking and thinking, common in the ancient world, in which ideas were arranged in a symmetrical pattern. Sometimes it involved, probably as an aid to memory, the pairing of thoughts in the following manner:

A   First idea
B   Second idea
B'   An idea similar to the second idea
A'   An idea similar to the first idea

This chiasmic pattern is intuitively employed today in modern speech. To use a contemporary illustration, the following paragraph is constructed in this A,B,B',A' chiasmic form:

> Ministers who have experienced difficult times in their own lives tend to be sensitive pastoral counselors (A), whereas ministers who have not suffered personally often lack deep compassion for the problems of others (B). When a minister has lived a relatively trouble-free life, he or she sometimes naively assumes that others should be able to manage their lives in the same carefree way (B'). Pastors who have felt pain themselves, however, recognize the wisdom in the saying that suffering is woven into the fabric of human life (A').

We can often observe this pattern at work in the body of a New Testament epistle. It is especially helpful to watch for this in the lengthy sections of a letter because it may clarify the structure of a seemingly convoluted passage. Consider the chiasmic structure of 1 Cor. 1:13—4:7.[12]

A   Is Christ divided? (1:13a)
B   Was Paul crucified for you? (1:13b)
C   Were you baptized in the name of Paul? (1:13b)
C'   Discussion of Paul and baptism (1:14-17)
B'   Discussion of Paul's preaching and the crucifixion of Christ (1:17—3:4)
A'   Discussion of the many servants and the one, undivided church (3:5—4:7)

There is a variation on this basic chiasmic pattern which has even more significance for reading and interpretation, the A,B,C,B',A' formula, a pattern that contains an unmatched element, C, at its center. This pattern at times signals that the key to the passage's meaning, the turning point, is to be found in the central unpaired element. Examples of this are common in contemporary language:

A The crisis: Since my wife died, I have struggled in a way that I had not imagined possible. The grief, the loneliness. There have been times when I did not know if I could make it.

B The transition: But through it all, I have discovered a new strength in my faith. In ways I cannot explain or even describe my prayer has become more earnest, my trust in God's love deeper.

A' The crisis restated: The grief has not gone away, and I still fight the loneliness, but I know now that I do not struggle alone.

The same transitional dynamic is found in 1 Cor. 12:4–30:[13]

A The variety of spiritual gifts (12:4–11)
B The one body (12:12–27)
A' The variety of gifts revisited (12:28–30)

The structure of this passage guides us inward to its center—the unity of the Body of Christ. First Paul names the issue, the variety of spiritual gifts. Next he moves to the heart of the matter, the unity of the Body of Christ. Then, in the third section, he returns to the original issue, but now this issue has been transformed by the new light given at the center of the discussion.

Closing

The ancient Greek letter typically ended with a word of "fare well," a statement expressing concern for the health and welfare of the recipients, and, on some occasions, secondary greetings (e.g., "Say hello to so and so"; "So and so sends greetings").[14] Paul, as we might expect, transforms these elements theologically. The "fare well" becomes a liturgical benediction, and the secondary greeting incorporates the vocabulary of Christian faith and worship ("Greet one another with a holy kiss"; "Greet every saint in Christ Jesus"). The endings of Paul's letters, in other words, evoked the never ending character of the communion of the saints.

How in particular does the text under consideration, in its own literary setting, embody the characteristics and dynamics described in the previous questions?

How may the sermon, in a new setting, say and do what the text says and does in its setting?

To see how this discussion can guide a preacher in moving from an epistolary text to a sermon, let us examine a representative text from the "body" section of 1 Corinthians. *1 Corinthians 12:31 — 14:1a.* First Corinthians 13 contains the well-known Pauline poem about love, a favorite passage at weddings. We must reach beyond the boundaries of chapter 13, however, to embrace the last phrase of chapter 12 and the first of chapter 14, for reasons which will become apparent later.

Examining the movement of 1 Corinthians as a whole, we see that this passage in the body or main section of the letter is a part of a larger section in which Paul answers questions asked by the Corinthians in an earlier letter. "Now concerning the matters about which you wrote," he begins (7:1) and off he goes with discussions of marriage, sexual morality, freedom, and worship. In chapter 12, Paul comes to the issue which will occupy him in the passage we will consider: "Now concerning spiritual gifts . . ."

Paul's response to this question from Corinth fills up three chapters of the letter, chapters 12—14. As Charles Talbert has noted, the section is patterned as a large chiasmus:[15]

A   Discussion of spiritual gifts (12:1–30)
B   Poetic section on love (12:31—14:1a)
A′   Discussion of spiritual gifts (14:1b–40)

In the light of this, we can already make some observations about the rhetorical effects of this passage upon its readers. First, the phrase "Now, concerning spiritual gifts" serves to remind the readers that

Paul writes in response to *their* question. In effect Paul is saying, "You wanted to know about spiritual gifts, so here it comes." This signals the reader to move into a question/answer mode: "We asked this; Paul answers that." Second, the chiasmic structure with the unpaired element in the center indicates that our particular passage, 1 Cor. 12:31—14:1a, may well serve as a transformational section, that is, as the heart of Paul's discussion.

As we follow the movement of the larger passage, we see that Paul repeats the topic of the readers' question and, for thirty verses or so, provides a response. As noted earlier, this part of the text has its own chiasmic structure. But the main thing to notice at this point is that chapter 12 provides an answer to the Corinthians' question and has a finished quality about it. Chapter 12 could, in fact, stand by itself, as if Paul were saying, "You asked a question. Here is the answer. Next question, please." But then, just as we anticipate his saying, "Next question," he surprises us by saying instead, "But earnestly desire the higher gifts. And I will show you a still more excellent way."

Notice what has happened here. Paul behaves as the teacher who hears the student's question, and provides a seemingly complete answer. But just as the satisfied student is turning the page in the notebook, ready to move on to the next topic, the teacher pauses, and says, "But let's get down to the *real* issue." There are, in other words, two answers to the question: the direct answer and the deeper answer, the answer that may cause the question itself to be redefined.

This deeper answer is given in 1 Cor. 12:31—14:1a, and when we look closely at its structure, we see that it, too, is a chiasmus.

A   The command to seek the "higher gift" (12:31)
B   The superiority of love (13:1-3)
C   The character of love (13:4-7)
B′ The superiority of love (13:8-13)
A′ The command to seek love (14:1a)

In order to follow the movement of this section, it is necessary to recall the situation at Corinth. The picture we get of the Corinthian congregation is of a young Christian congregation vibrating with the electricity of the Spirit. Speaking in tongues, prophetic utterances, healings—these and more were the marks of worship at Corinth. The

Lord's Day at Corinth was undoubtedly exciting, but the problem they had with all this—and here is the source of the question sent to Paul—was that a competitive and very human spirit had become mixed in with these manifestations of the Holy Spirit. Whose gift was the highest and the best? Whose gift was to be given the privilege of the floor in worship? These issues were at the root of much of the division in Corinth.

In the section of the letter we have already examined (1 Cor. 12:1-30), Paul had given his direct answer: spiritual gifts are like parts of the body, all equal and all necessary, and you are the Body of Christ. But now he leads into the second and deeper answer with a line full of irony: "But earnestly desire the higher gifts." The irony in this is that "desiring the higher gifts," jockeying for spiritual advantage, is precisely the Corinthians' problem. Having apparently answered their question with a full and finished answer which dismissed the categories of "higher" and "lower," Paul now surprises his readers by saying more, and tantalizes them by reopening the forbidden notion of a "higher gift."

But watch what happens. "If I speak in the tongues of human beings and angels," Paul begins, and the tongue speakers at Corinth bask momentarily in the spotlight. Only momentarily, however, for Paul continues, "But have not love, I am a noisy gong or a clanging cymbal." In terms of rhetorical effect, Paul has summoned forth the tongue speakers, given them an instant of glorious recognition, and then suddenly pulled the carpet out from under them by calling into question the adequacy of their gift. A pattern thus established, Paul proceeds methodically to spotlight each group at Corinth: "If I have prophetic powers," "If I understand all mysteries and all knowledge," "If I have all faith," "If I give my body." Each group leans forward on cue only to hear the verdict, "But have not love, I am nothing."

If Paul had been present in the flesh, pointing his finger at the Corinthians as they worshiped, the moment may well have proved too intense. There probably would have been more shame than growth. The freedom of the letter form protected the Corinthians from the full glare of Paul's presence and gave to them at least the possibility of receiving what was to come next.

Having moved around the congregation group by group and raised the awareness that without love they are all for nought, Paul now moves to the center of the chiasmus, to the heart of the matter. "Love is patient . . . kind . . . not jealous or boastful." On and on goes the description of love. Paul is describing not some new and higher spiritual gift, one which the Corinthians can scramble over each other to pursue, but an attitude, a way of common life through which all gifts are to be expressed. This section transforms the original quest to discover the proper ranking of gifts and deepens the notion of equality portrayed in the body image by investing it with the active dynamic of love. Paul's language is creative and poetic. It does more than simply give the Corinthians data about love; it creates the reality of love in their hearing. Love becomes so close, so palpable, they can reach out and touch it, claim it for themselves if they would.

And if they do, the Corinthians can bear, as never before, hearing that all of their vaunted and jealously claimed spiritual gifts are not only partial and incomplete but imperfect and temporary: they will "pass away." Each group had thought of its gift as a sign that it somehow stood above the other groups. More than that, they had viewed their gifts as the end, the goal, of the Christian life. "This is what life in Christ is all about," they had thought. Now Paul is telling them that their gifts are simply the means for moving *toward* something else, something truly lasting: faith, hope, and especially love. The Corinthians came to Paul with a question to be answered, a dispute to be settled, a conflict to be negotiated. He gives them instead a new horizon, a shared direction, and a common end: "Make love your aim."

So, far from being simply a gentle poem for a wedding day, this is a preaching text for fierce church conflict, for those times when congregations cry out, "How do we heal this painful division?"

How should a sermon on the text be developed? The possibilities are many, of course, but one option would be to follow the rhetorical development of the text itself. Almost every congregation includes within it rival and heartfelt understandings of the Gospel, even competitive notions of spiritual "gifts" and ministries. A sermon could begin by fairly and evocatively describing some of these and then go on to ask the inevitable questions, Which is the best? Which vision of the Gospel and the church's life is to be honored above the others? The first response is the one initially given by Paul: there are varieties of gifts, ministries, and understandings of the Gospel, but there is but one Spirit who inspires them all. They all work together, like the parts of the body. Good question; good answer.

The sermon could then move on, as did the text, to change the very way in which the question was posed. The real question, the deeper issue, is not Whose agenda should claim the church's attention? but What is *any* agenda worth if it lacks love? The sermon, if it is true to the rhetorical effect of the passage, will be a bold one, and will name names. "If I have been given the gift of a passion for justice, but have not love . . ." "If I have the gift of telling the gospel to the unchurched, but have not love . . ." "If I am given the commitment to tithe and read a book of the Bible every day, but have not love . . ." "If I have been led to withhold my income tax in protest for the cause of peace, but have not love . . ."

If the sermon works as the passage in Paul's letter did, it will not lead the congregation to devalue or abandon any serious project, cause, or expression of ministry. Rather, it will call the congregation and help enable it to envision each member as moving toward and therefore being shaped by the deeper dynamic and goal of Christian love. "Make love your aim . . ."

8
SERMON
notes

regenerate the biblical text

THE STONE THROWN INTO THE POND

In chapter 2 I stated that the preacher's task is not to *replicate* the biblical text but to *regenerate* the impact of some portion of that text. In this sense the biblical text is like a stone tossed into a pond. Its immediate impact is felt where it falls—the historical situation into which it originally landed—but this impact creates ripples which flow in time across the surface. As the ripples move away from the center in ever-expanding circles, their motion is impelled by the original event of the text, but their shape is altered as they strike objects in the water and blend with other waves. The task of preaching is not merely to recover the text's original breaking of the surface but to express what happens when one of the ripples sent forth by that text crosses our spot in the pond.

we are in a ripple

This involves an act of faithful imagination on the part of the preacher. There are methods for reading and understanding the biblical text, but ultimately no method can accomplish the task of discerning the claims made by a text upon a new situation and a different set of hearers. Only the preacher as interpreter, by knowing well both text and contemporary situation, can do that. Moreover, the engagement between a biblical text and a new occasion for hearing creates not one but many possibilities for the sermon.

Imagine that you have attended a performance of a powerful play which moved you deeply. The next day a friend asks, "How was the play?" Now what you want to do, of course, is to tell your friend more than facts about the performance. You want your friend to

experience at least a taste of the play's energy. Having been moved by
what you saw and heard, you want your friend to connect in some
way with your intensity. How do you respond? What can you say to
the question, "How was the play?"

Perhaps you will reenact the dialogue of a particularly evocative
scene. Maybe you will summarize the plot, recite a line that made you
laugh or squirm, or try to put into your own words the insights
you gained from the play. What you are after is recreating the play's
impact, and there are many approaches you can take to do this. The
one you choose will naturally depend upon the kind of play you saw,
but it will also depend upon the kind of people you and your friend
happen to be.

Preaching on a biblical text embraces the same choices and the same
dynamics. "How was the text?" the congregation tacitly inquires, and
the creation of the sermon involves a searching at the intersection of
text, preacher, and new situation for the apt form and the best words
to tell them.

FROM FORCE TO FORM

The text-to-sermon examples at the close of the chapters on the
literary forms suggest several paths from text to sermon. There are,
of course, many other possibilities for allowing the force of a biblical
text to be expressed through a sermon form. Indeed, every sermon
should be "custom-made" since it arises out of an encounter between the specific text and a new situation. The following list describes in more detail four broad types of text-to-sermon bonds that
were briefly mentioned before. It is by no means a complete list, but
rather the initial steps toward a much longer and richer set of
choices.

Allow the Movement of the Sermon to
Follow the Movement
of the Text

Sometimes we can take our cues as to how the sermon should
proceed from the inner sequences of the text itself, a possibility described in the discussion of the parables of the Treasure and the Pearl
(chapter 6). This approach is especially appropriate with narrative
texts where meaning is developed partially through the movement of

plot. The sermon can be fashioned so that its movements mirror the unfolding of the originating narrative.

Consider, for example, the story of Elijah and the priests of Baal (1 Kings 18:17–40). One way to preach on this text (only one, it should be reiterated) is to create a sermon whose structure matches the episodes of the plot. In order to do this, we need to make a decision about the narrative point of entry. How does the reader enter into this story? The way in which a narrator tells a story creates a certain relationship between the reader and the story, and, in the case of 1 Kings, the narrator has established a sympathetic relationship between the reader and the principal character Elijah. This narrative comes as one of a string of Elijah stories in which the prophet is presented positively, the result of which is to place the reader squarely in Elijah's camp. The reader wants Elijah to succeed—whatever that may mean—and in a literary sense the reader identifies with Elijah.

How does the plot, seen from Elijah's vantage point, unfold? Here are four main movements:

1. *Charge and Countercharge.* Accused of being a "troubler of Israel" (18:17), Elijah issues a countercharge of idolatry (18:18).
2. *The Test Arranged.* Elijah sets up a contest with the prophets of Baal (18:19–25).
3. *The Critique of False Prophecy.* Elijah mockingly watches as Baal's prophets fail (18:26–29).
4. *The Invocation and the Manifestation.* Elijah calls upon God who answers in dramatic fashion, thereby provoking awe and worship and causing the condemnation of the false prophets (18:30–40).

Notice that the four plot movements have all been phrased in terms of their relationship to Elijah. The sermon now traces these same four movements as it calls upon the hearers both to focus upon Elijah's role in this story and to view their own world with Elijah-like vision. Here is a schematic of how the sermon structure may unfold:

1. In the opening section of the sermon, the hearers are accused, like Elijah, of being "troublers of Israel." How, in our day, does a congregation of Christian people trouble the larger society? By calling for peace in a war-making world? By insisting that every person is a child of God and worthy of dignity and care in a culture ready to write certain people off as worthless? By using words like "sin" instead of

"miscalculation," "grace" instead of "luck"? By pointing to the mystery of God in a technological age? The possible responses are many, but they all signal a recognition that the church's life is gathered around the reality of the living God who has been replaced in the culture by more proximate and less demanding deities.

2. The church does not, of course, set up an altar in the public square and invite a showdown with the culture, but there are contests out there nonetheless. Who defines what it means to be human? Who are our neighbors? Are we our brothers' and sisters' keepers? What does it mean for society genuinely to be productive? What power can truly save us? These and other questions form the altars around which rival priests gather.

3. We may not mock as Elijah did, but we can observe with a critical eye all the ministrations of false priests. The human potential movement calls out to the god of self, but we are left as lonely and restless as before. "Perhaps your god is on vacation," says Elijah. The high priests of education call out to the god of knowledge, "Society's problems are a result of a lack of data and information. Surely when the fire of knowledge comes down upon us, clarity will provide redemption." And we end up educated but still broken, or, as Walker Percy noted, "making A's but flunking life." "Perhaps your god is asleep in class," jests Elijah—for clarity and knowledge, with all their value and power, finally cannot save us either.

4. At this point in the Elijah story, the prophet called upon the name of God and the altar was consumed in fire, provoking awe and worship.

The task of the sermon now is to point to those places in our own experiences in which the presence of the true and saving God is manifest and which prompt our awe and worship. While one may wish for an epiphany as forceful as flames devouring the waterlogged wood of Elijah's altar, God's presence is rarely if ever experienced so unambiguously. We must point instead to more subtle epiphanies. Robert McAfee Brown tells of worshiping in a Lutheran church in East Berlin just before the Berlin Wall was erected. During the service a young couple presented their child for baptism, an act of courage since the government policy discouraged religious practice and had developed secular rituals to replace those of the church. Nevertheless, this couple, jeopardizing their own future, had brought their child to be baptized. In a way they were reenacting the Elijah story. The state prophets had their rituals, but this couple found those ceremonies empty and powerless. They chose instead to claim God's promises for their child. The moment revealed, said Brown, "their quiet, public courage." But something else was revealed as well. The faith of this couple pointed to the presence of the living and saving God and to the truth about their child that transcended all the incantations of the state: "This is surely a child of God."[1]

Even though the possibility of matching sermonic movement to text movement is clearest when the biblical text is a narrative, non-narrative texts possess their own inner movements that can also serve as the patterns for sermons. In Ps. 19:7–10, for example, the psalmist employs the technique of parallelism to praise the Torah, the central teaching of the faith. The verses come at us like measured drum beats: "the *law* of the Lord," "the *testimony* of the Lord," "the *precepts* of the Lord," "the *commandments* of the Lord." These terms are almost but not quite synonymous. Each describes the Torah, but each construes it in its own way, and with special virtue and benefit: "perfect, reviving the soul," "sure, making wise the simple," "right, rejoicing the heart," "pure, enlightening the eyes." The movement of the text, then, is march-like in cadence and advance, and its rhetorical impact is to invite the reader to fall in step.

This psalm, therefore, provides the opportunity to create a sermon that does more than name the many ways by which we describe the truth of the faith (e.g., law; gospel; testimony; good news; teachings of the faith; old, old, story). It not only fleshes out the power of that truth in our lives (e.g., revives our souls; renews our hope; turns our foolishness into wisdom; creates joy; opens our eyes to human need) but also marches in rhythmic drumbeat fashion, inviting the hearer finally to join in the march. Instead of "The third thing I want to say about the truth of the Christian faith," the congregation would hear a series of similar but not identical refrains punctuating the movements of the sermon: "The law of the Lord is perfect, reviving the soul." "The good news of the gospel is sure, renewing our hope." "The old, old story of God's way with the world is true, calling us to justice."

Allow the Opposing Forces in the Text to Become the Opposing Forces in the Sermon

Some biblical texts pit opposing forces, ways of living, or visions of the world against each other, thereby calling upon the reader to make a choice. The sermon can regenerate this conflict and its accompanying call for decision. This possibility was described in the discussion of Psalm 1 (chapter 3), in which by means of images the way of the righteous is set against the way of the wicked.

Another example of this kind of text is the story of Zacchaeus (Luke 19:1-10). Near the end of the story the reader is given two contrasting pictures: the disgusted, murmuring crowd all in a snit because Jesus has "gone in to be the guest of a man who is a sinner" (v. 7), and Zacchaeus himself, joyfully cutting loose his wealth (v. 8). A careful reading reveals that these scenes do not occur one after the other so much as simultaneously. The crowd and Zacchaeus are on stage at the same time, and the reader sees both the bitter crowd at stage left and the exuberant Zacchaeus at stage right. Sniping and giving happen in the same moment, and the reader wonders, "Where would I rather be, outside with the crowd or inside with Zacchaeus and Jesus?"

One possibility for the sermon, then, is for the preacher to find contemporary examples of both the murmuring of the crowd and the joyful, freeing release of Zacchaeus under the power of the Gospel. The sermon would involve (1) presenting in vivid fashion these two ways of being and living, "on the one hand, and on the other" so to speak, and (2) issuing the invitation to the hearers to choose where they would rather be.

Allow the Central Insight of the Text to Be the Central Insight of the Sermon

Some texts are designed to interact with readers in such a way that the readers discover and learn an insight, truth, or idea. (See the discussions of Prov. 15:17, chapter 4, and the Book of Ruth, chapter 5). Here the task of the sermon becomes teaching this idea and exploring its ramifications for the hearers.

For example, one of the many dynamics present in Matt. 1:18–25, the story of Joseph and the birth of Jesus, is a teaching about the meaning of true righteousness. After setting the scene, the narrator concentrates the reader's attention on Joseph. We are directly told that Joseph was a "just man," and are given concrete evidence of his character: "Unwilling to put her to shame, he resolved to divorce her quietly." At this point in the story, being just—Joseph-style—has two qualities: knowledge of the just thing to do and a determination to do it with compassion.

As the story unfolds, however, this notion of being just gets changed—not replaced, but transformed. The message of Joseph's dream is that he does not, as a matter of fact, really know what he must do to be just. The voice of the Lord gives him a new and unexpected assignment: "Joseph, son of David, do not fear to take Mary your wife, for that which is conceived in her is of the Holy Spirit." Now the dilemma before Joseph is this: Does a just person always do what the code of ethics prescribes, albeit with compassion, or does a just person remain open to a new movement of the Spirit, however surprising? Is a just person obedient to the law because it is the law, or is a just person obedient to the law because it attunes one to the living voice of God which demands a deeper obedience?

Joseph made his decision. "When Joseph woke from sleep, he did as the angel of the Lord commanded him." The text then works to give the reader a new understanding of being just that does not merely apply set principles to new situations but seeks to discern the will of God in each new moment and to be obedient to that. This is not all that the text does, but it does teach this truth, and a sermon on this text may well be a teaching sermon aimed at communicating this insight. Such a sermon may explore contemporary situations in which the church and Christian people are called upon to perform the right and just action. How do we decide what that action should be? Do we appeal to precedent as though we already know what the good should be, or do we prayerfully explore the tradition and open ourselves to a fresh movement of the Spirit, seeking to discern the will of God for this day and this situation?

Allow the Mood of the Text
to Set the Mood
of the Sermon

Biblical texts impart more than feelings, of course, but part of the rhetorical impact of a text, and thus its meaning, has to do with the emotional mood it creates. The words "praise God," for example, mean something different when they are sung in a joyous doxology than when they are barked out as a command. We encountered the power of mood in the discussions of Phil. 2:5–11 (chapter 2) and the thanksgiving sections of the epistles (chapter 7). One teacher of homiletics advises students, as a step in exegesis, to imagine appropriate music for the biblical text. Trying to decide whether the text is better accompanied by a flute or a trombone can go a long way toward determining the text's mood.

A sermon on 1 Cor. 10:14–22, for instance, may well pick up on the quiet, "come let us reason together" style of the text. "Judge for yourselves," "Is this not so?" "Consider this," the text calmly encourages the reader. This text is definitely a sonata for flute and violin. Revelation 19, however, with its vision of the thundering multitudes in heaven shouting, "Hallelujah!" demands a full orchestra with kettle drum and cymbals. Preaching on this text may well mean reciting poetry, quoting hymns, employing grand images—anything to regenerate the mood of awe and wonder so central to the text itself.

CANT AND CANTATA

This list of linkages between text and sermon ends not with a period, but an ellipsis. It is now up to the preacher to supply more of the countless creative ways that sermons can sing to the tunes played by biblical texts.

"Creative," however, is a word preachers ought to use with care. In preaching, creativity has little to do with inventiveness and everything to do with faithfulness to what the Spirit creates through the text. If the preacher does not read the text diligently before writing and listen to the text attentively before speaking, creativity becomes mere cleverness and that cherished harmony between text and sermon is reduced to a thin, discordant solo. The hope is for a cantata; the temptation is to produce cant.

In other words, the means should not be mistaken for the end. Biblical texts are not *about* literary genre and rhetorical strategies. Rather they employ genre and rhetoric to witness to the event of God-with-us. We are not finished with these texts when we have assayed their literary features. Better yet, these texts are not finished with us until we have glimpsed the holy horizon toward which they point.

Any separation between a theological experiencing of biblical texts and a literary understanding of them is, in the words of George Steiner, "radically factitious. It cannot work." In considering the essential difference between the Bible and other literary classics, Steiner states,

> I can—just—come to imagine for myself that a man of more or less my own biological and social composition could have written *Hamlet* or *Lear* and gone home to lunch and found a normal answer to the question "How did it go today?" I cannot conceive of the author of the "Speech Out of the Whirlwind" in Job writing or dictating that text and dwelling within the common existence and parlance.[2]

So the biblical texts sing not a ballad but a hymn, not a lullaby but an awestruck *sanctus*. And preachers must fall to the ground crying, "Woe is me! For I am lost," before being lifted by grace and placed among the choir singing the ceaseless anthem of the ages.

notes

1. LEARNING HOW TO READ

1. The poem is "The Man He Killed" by Thomas Hardy. The discussion regarding the device of repetition is suggested by Laurence Perrine in *Sound and Sense: An Introduction to Poetry*, 2d ed. (New York: Harcourt, Brace & World, 1963), 20–21.

2. Stanley Fish, *Is There a Text in This Class?* (Cambridge: Harvard University Press, 1980), 168.

3. Robert Scholes, *Textual Power: Literary Theory and the Teaching of English* (New Haven: Yale University Press, 1985), 21–22.

4. Bliss Perry, *A Study of Poetry* (Boston: Houghton Mifflin, 1920), 155.

5. Wolfgang Iser, "Interaction Between Text and Reader," in *The Reader in the Text*, ed. Susan R. Suleiman and Inge Crosman (Princeton: Princeton University Press, 1980), 110.

2. MOVING FROM TEXT TO SERMON

1. John H. Hayes and Carl R. Holladay, *Biblical Exegesis: A Beginner's Handbook* (Atlanta: John Knox Press, 1982), 24.

2. John Barton, *Reading the Old Testament: Method in Biblical Study* (Philadelphia: Westminster Press, 1984), 32.

3. This limerick is found in Perrine, *Sound and Sense: An Introduction to Poetry*, 204.

4. Fish, *Is There a Text In This Class?* 14.

5. Ibid., 326–27.

6. Robert Scholes, *Textual Power: Literary Theory and the Teaching of English*, 158–59.

7. Ibid., 161.

8. Paul Ricoeur, "The Hermeneutical Function of Distanciation," in *Hermeneutics and the Social Sciences*, ed. and trans. John B. Thompson. (Cambridge: Cambridge University Press, 1981), 139.

9. Kenneth Grayston, *The Letters of Paul to the Philippians and to the Thessalonians*, The Cambridge Bible Commentary of the New English Bible (Cambridge: Cambridge University Press, 1967), esp. 20–26.

10. Robert Alter, *The Art of Biblical Narrative: A Literary Approach to the Bible* (New York: Basic Books, 1981), 21.

3. PREACHING ON THE PSALMS

1. Patrick D. Miller, Jr., *Interpreting the Psalms* (Philadelphia: Fortress Press, 1986), 20.

2. Claus Westermann, *Praise and Lament in the Psalms*, trans. Keith R. Crim and Richard N. Soulen (Atlanta: John Knox Press, 1981), 19–35.

3. Laurence Perrine, *Sound and Sense: An Introduction to Poetry*, 24.

4. Ibid., 10–11.

5. Walter Brueggemann, "Psalms and the Life of Faith: A Suggested Typology of Function," in *Journal for the Study of the Old Testament*, vol. 17 (1980), 4.

6. Ibid., 7–9. Brueggemann divides the Psalter into three hermeneutical categories which he derives from the work of Paul Ricoeur: orientation, dislocation, and reorientation.

7. Laurence Perrine, *Sound and Sense: An Introduction to Poetry*, 3–4.

8. Robert Alter, *The Art of Biblical Poetry* (New York: Basic Books, 1985), 113.

9. Ibid., 113–14.

10. Miller, *Interpreting the Psalms*, 30.

11. Ibid., 31.

12. Ibid.

13. T. H. Robinson, *The Poetry of the Old Testament*, as quoted in Alter, *The Art of Biblical Poetry*, 9.

14. James Kugel, *The Idea of Biblical Poetry* (New Haven: Yale University Press, 1981).

15. Kugel, as quoted in Miller, *Interpreting the Psalms*, 33.

16. Alter, *The Art of Biblical Poetry*, 115–18.

17. Ibid., 115.

18. Ibid., 116.

19. Miller, *Interpreting the Psalms*, 82.

20. Alter, *The Art of Biblical Poetry*, 116–17.

21. Miller, *Interpreting the Psalms*, 85.

22. Judith Guest, *Ordinary People* (New York: Ballantine Books, 1976), 47.

4. PREACHING ON PROVERBS

1. William McKane (*Proverbs: A New Approach*, The Old Testament Library [Philadelphia: Westminster Press, 1970], 11) has suggested that those proverbs which exhibit God-language are actually reinterpretations of older, more "secular" proverbs and reflect a later stage in the Old Testament wisdom tradition.

2. The biblical Book of Proverbs contains literature representative of several literary genres. The sort of text we will be considering, and calling a "proverb," is the brief epigram that McKane terms the "individual wisdom sentence." Ibid., 10.

3. David Jasper, *The New Testament and the Literary Imagination* (Atlantic Highlands, N.J.: Humanities Press International, 1987), 74.

4. Ibid., 74–75.

5. James G. Williams, *Those Who Ponder Proverbs: Aphoristic Thinking and Biblical Literature* (Sheffield, Eng.: The Almond Press, 1981), 80.

6. Ibid., 14.

7. Paul Ricoeur, "Biblical Hermeneutics," *Semeia* 4 (1975): 113.

8. McKane, *Proverbs: A New Approach*, 23.

9. Ibid., 23.

10. Ibid.

11. Alter, *The Art of Biblical Poetry*, 169.

12. The example proverbs are from the *Good News Bible: Today's English Version* (New York: The American Bible Society, 1971).

13. Garrison Keillor, *Lake Wobegon Days* (New York: Viking Press, 1985), 248–49.

5. PREACHING ON NARRATIVES

1. Adele Berlin, *Poetics and Biblical Interpretation* (Sheffield, Eng.: The Almond Press, 1983), 11.

2. Reynolds Price, *A Palpable God* (New York: Atheneum, 1978), 14.

3. Robert Alter, *The Art of Biblical Narrative*, 33.

4. Ibid.

5. Ibid., 157–59.

6. Meir Sternberg, *The Poetics of Biblical Narrative: Ideological Reading and the Drama of Reading* (Bloomington, Ind.: Indiana University Press, 1985), 41.

7. Ibid., 41–44.

8. Sternberg, *The Poetics of Biblical Narrative*, 46–47.

9. Robert Scholes, *Structuralism in Literature: An Introduction* (New Haven: Yale University Press, 1974), 95.

10. I recognize that the very traditional notion of narrative described here has been challenged by modern fiction, some of which, for example, sets up tensions which are not resolved in the endings. I am content with the traditional model, however, because biblical narratives generally conform to this pattern.

11. This tale, from the Hasidic School of Pshiskhe, was recounted by Belden C. Lane, "Rabbinical Stories: A Primer on Theological Method," *The Christian Century* 98, no. 41 (December 16, 1981): 1309.

12. Walker Percy, *Lost in the Cosmos: The Last Self-Help Book* (New York: Farrar, Straus & Giroux, 1983), 7.

13. Amos Wilder, *The Language of the Gospel: Early Christian Rhetoric* (New York: Harper & Row, 1964), 65.

14. Norman N. Holland, *5 Readers Reading* (New Haven and London: Yale University Press, 1975), 205.

15. Robert C. Tannehill, "Introduction: The Pronouncement Story and Its Types," *Semeia* 20 (1981): 3.

16. Berlin, *Poetic and Biblical Interpretation*, 36.

17. Alter, *The Art of Biblical Narrative*, 44.

6. PREACHING ON THE PARABLES OF JESUS

1. Norman Perrin, *Jesus and the Language of the Kingdom* (Philadelphia: Fortress Press, 1976), 93.

2. C. H. Dodd, *The Parables of the Kingdom* (London and Glasgow: Fontana Books, 1961), 16.

3. Paul Ricoeur, "Biblical Hermeneutics," *Semeia* 4 (1975): 114-18.

4. Joachim Jeremias, *The Parables of Jesus* (New York: Charles Scribner's Sons, 1963). See especially section 2.

5. See Matthew Black, "The Parables as Allegory," *The Bulletin of the John Rylands Library* 42 (1959-60): 273-87; and Raymond E. Brown, "Parable and Allegory Reconsidered," *Novum Testamentum* 5 (1962): 36-45.

6. Perrin, *Jesus and the Language of the Kingdom*, 202.

7. Robert W. Funk, *Language, Hermeneutic, and Word of God* (New York: Harper & Row, 1966), 212.

8. Ibid., 214.

9. John Drury, *The Parables in the Gospels* (New York: Crossroad Press, 1985), 64.

10. Jack Dean Kingsbury, *The Parables of Jesus in Matthew 13* (London: SPCK, 1969), 130.

11. John Dominic Crossan, *In Parables* (New York: Harper & Row, 1973), 34-36.

12. Dan Wakefield, "Returning to Church," *The New York Times Magazine* (December 22, 1985): 16-17, 22-28.

13. Ibid., 26.

7. PREACHING ON EPISTLES

1. William G. Doty, *Letters in Primitive Christianity* (Philadelphia: Fortress Press, 1973), 19.

2. Ibid.

3. Ibid., 44.

4. The notion of the relationship between closeness and distance in letters, as well as some of the other ideas about letters in this chapter, were stimulated through conversations with Fred B. Craddock.

5. Doty, *Letters in Primitive Christianity*, 24-26.

6. Ibid., 21-22.

7. Heikki Koskenniemi, *Studien zur Idee und Phraseologie des griechischen Briefes bis 400 n. Chr.* (Helsinki: Suomalaien Tiedeakatemie, 1956). Koskenniemi's findings are summarized in Doty, *Letters in Primitive Christianity*, 10ff.

8. Doty, *Letters in Primitive Christianity*, 42.

9. Ibid., 80.

10. Ibid., 29.

11. George A. Kennedy, *New Testament Interpretation Through Rhetorical Criticism* (Chapel Hill, N.C.: University of North Carolina Press, 1984), 19 *et passim*. Kennedy found that in terms of rhetorical "type," some of the Pauline epistolary material is *judicial* (most of 2 Corinthians), some is *deliberative* (Galatians), and some is *epideictic* (Romans). Judicial rhetoric seeks "to persuade the audience to make a judgment about events occurring in the past," deliberative rhetoric desires "to persuade them to take some action in the future," and epideictic rhetoric "seeks to persuade them to hold or reaffirm some point of view in the present." Each type of rhetoric employs its own conventional structure and pattern of argument.

12. See Charles H. Talbert, *Reading Corinthians: A Literary and Theological Commentary on 1 and 2 Corinthians* (New York: Crossroad Publishing, 1987), 4–9.

13. See Talbert, *Reading Corinthians*, 82.

14. John L. White, "The Ancient Epistolography Group in Retrospect," *Semeia* 22 (1981): 9.

15. Talbert, *Reading Corinthians*, 81.

8. SERMON NOTES

1. Robert McAfee Brown, *Creative Dislocation* (Nashville: Abingdon Press, 1980), 19.

2. George Steiner, "Books: The Good Book," *The New Yorker* (January 11, 1988): 97.

INDEX
of names and subjects

141

INDEX
of biblical texts

143